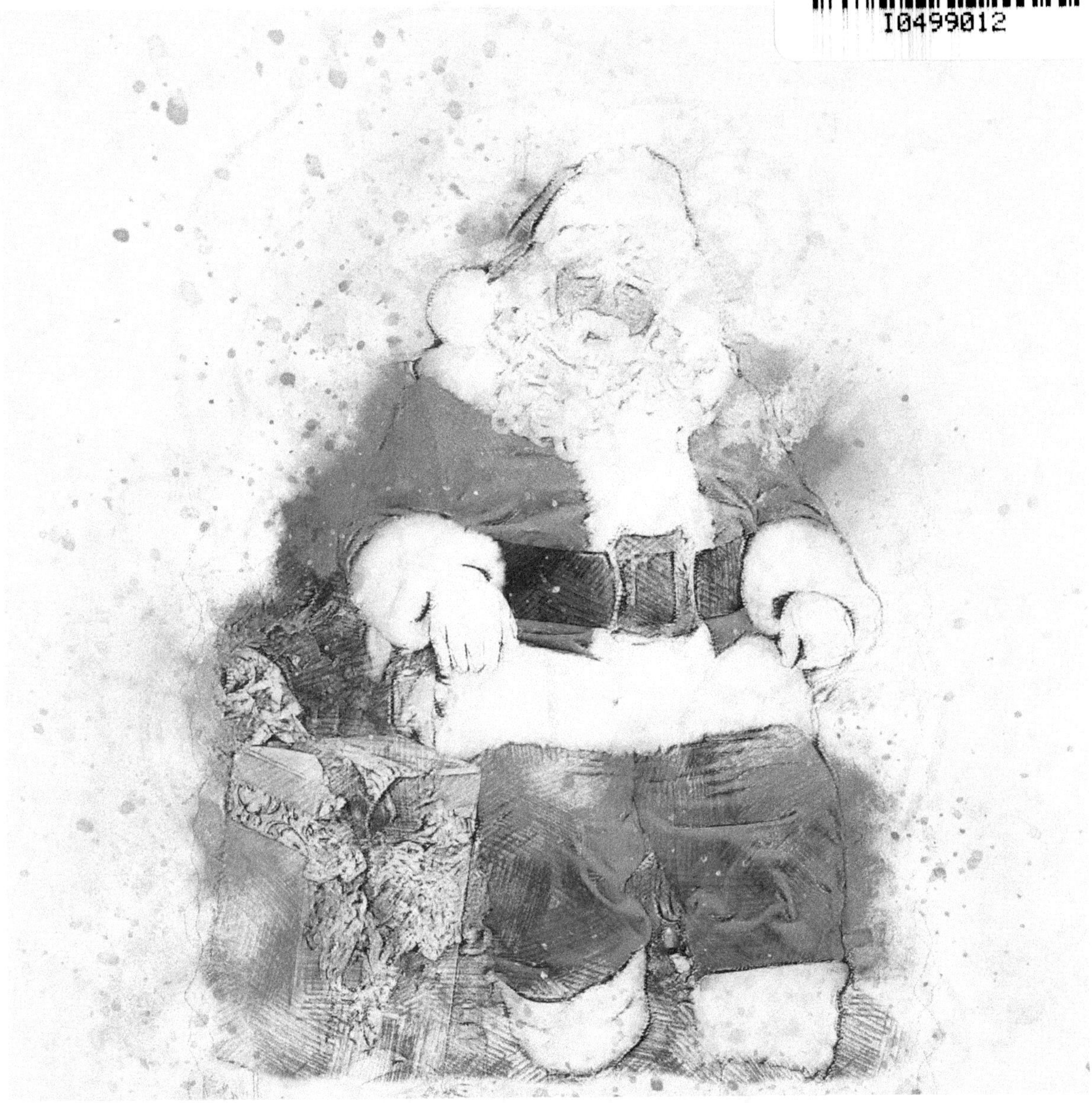

2019

david perry

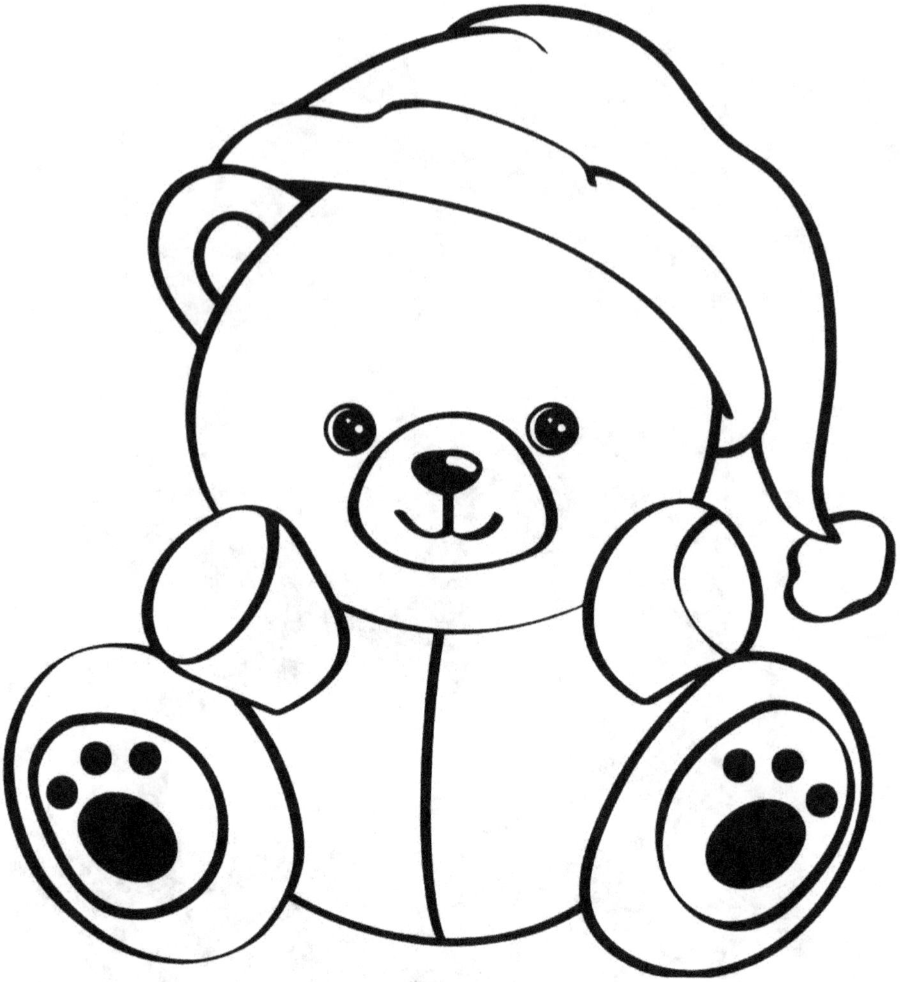

This Book Belongs to :

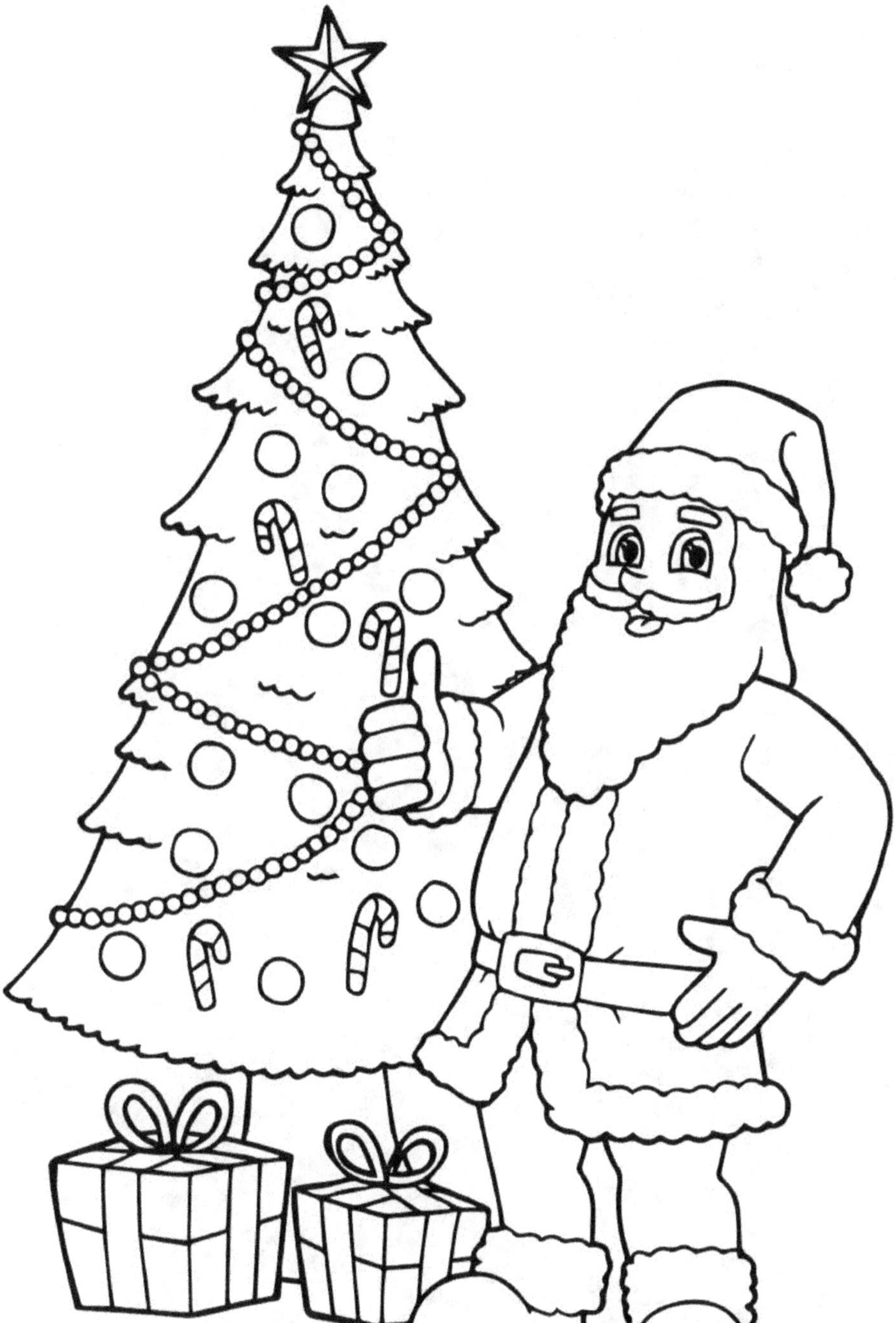

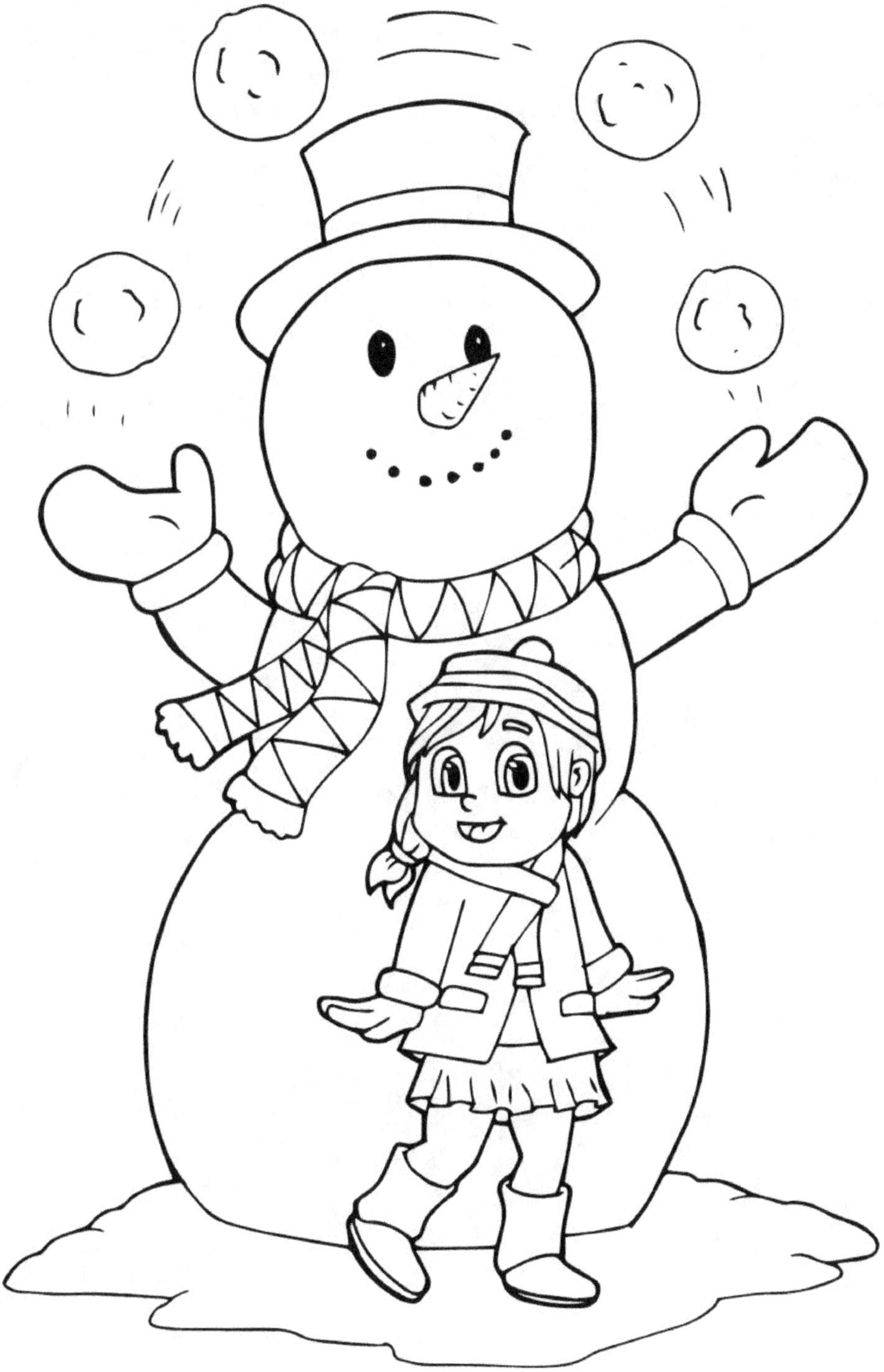

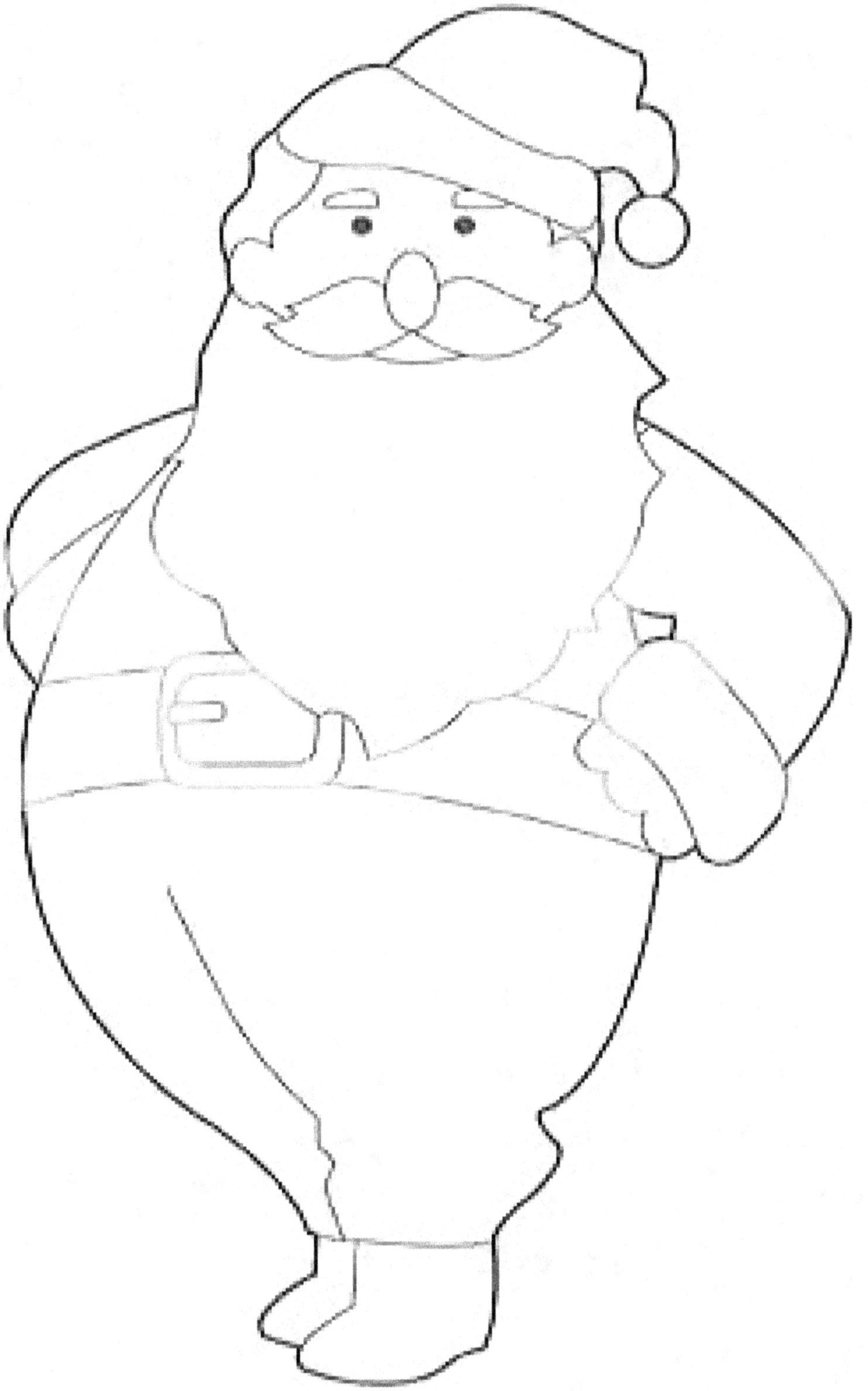

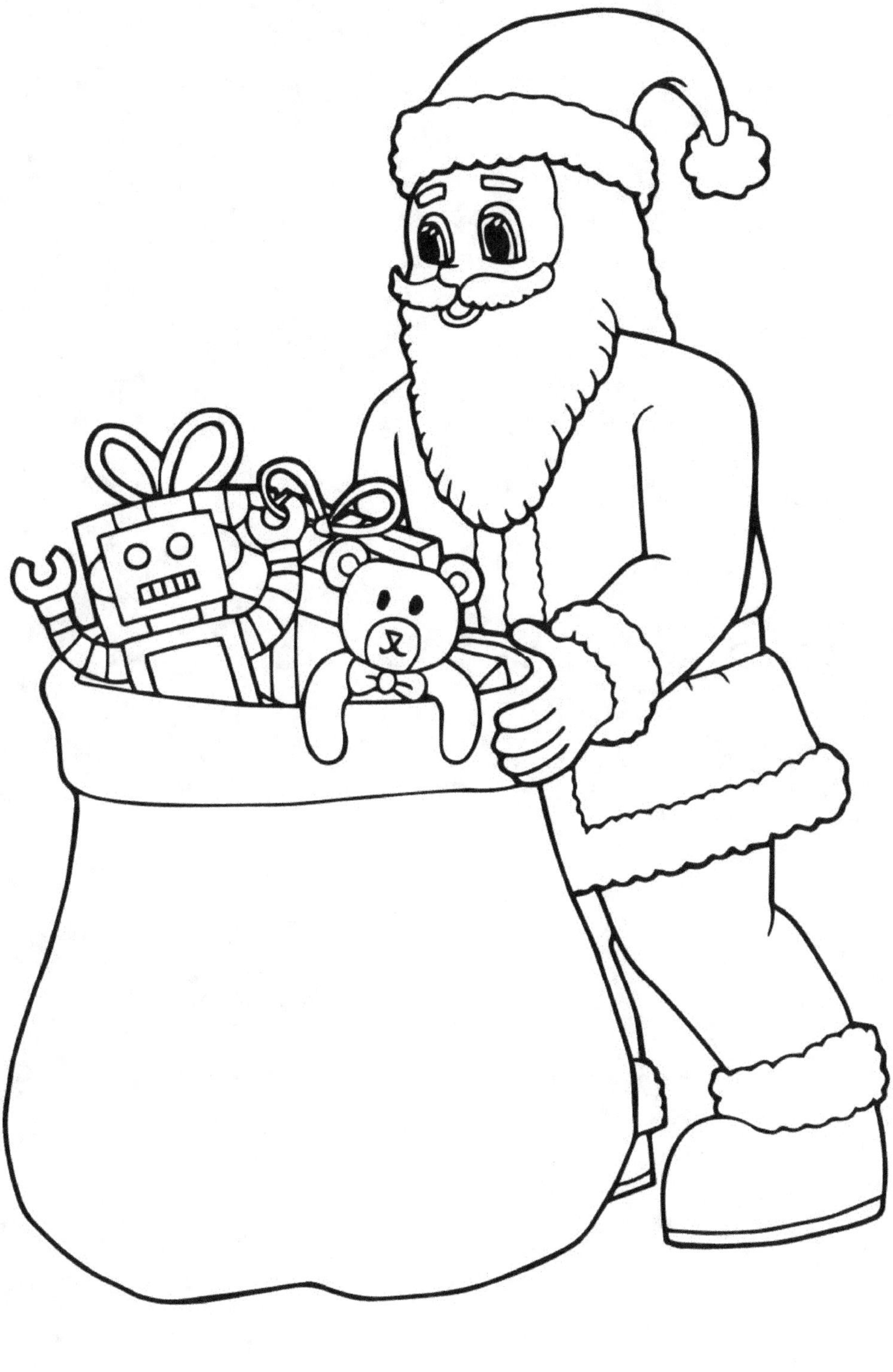

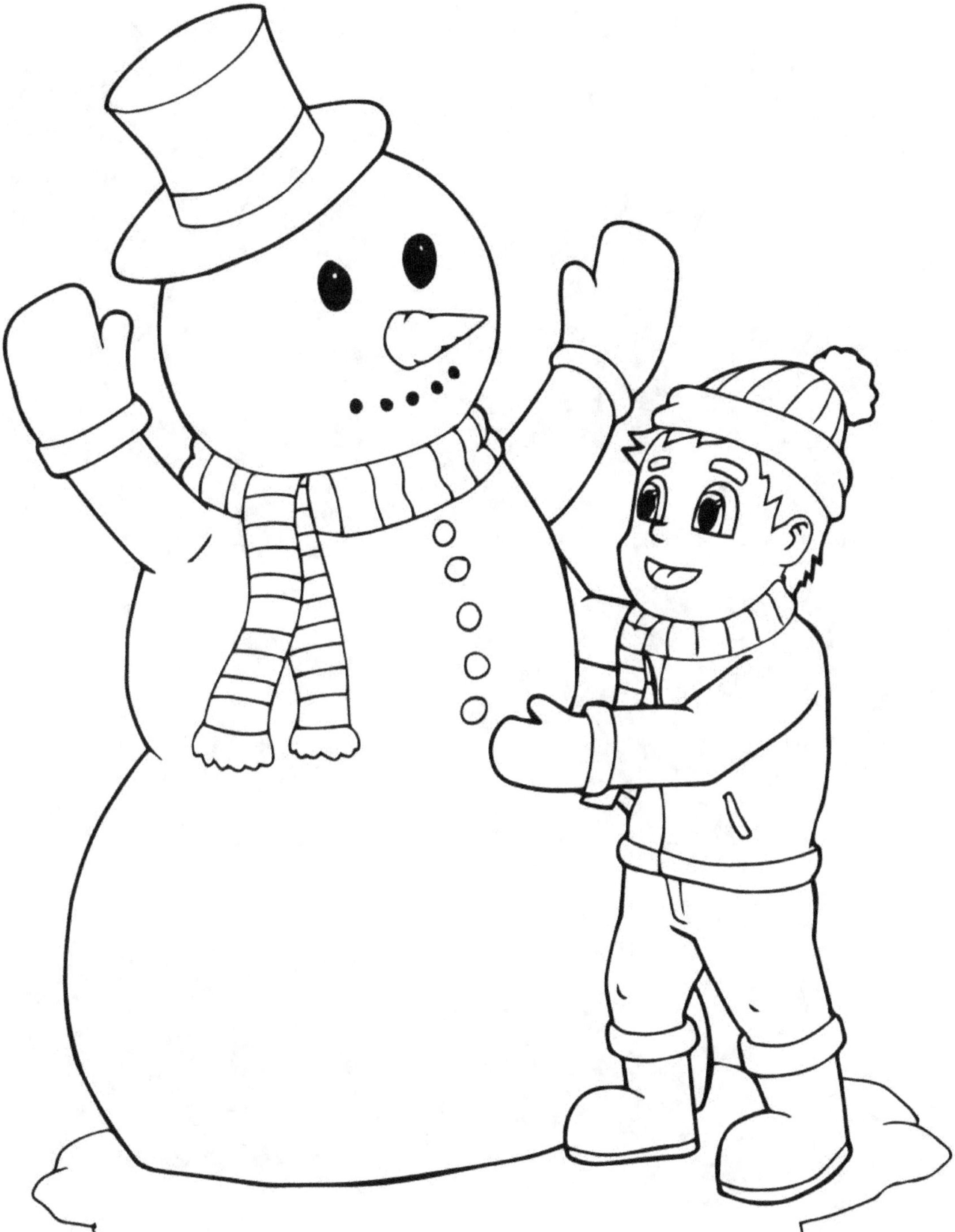

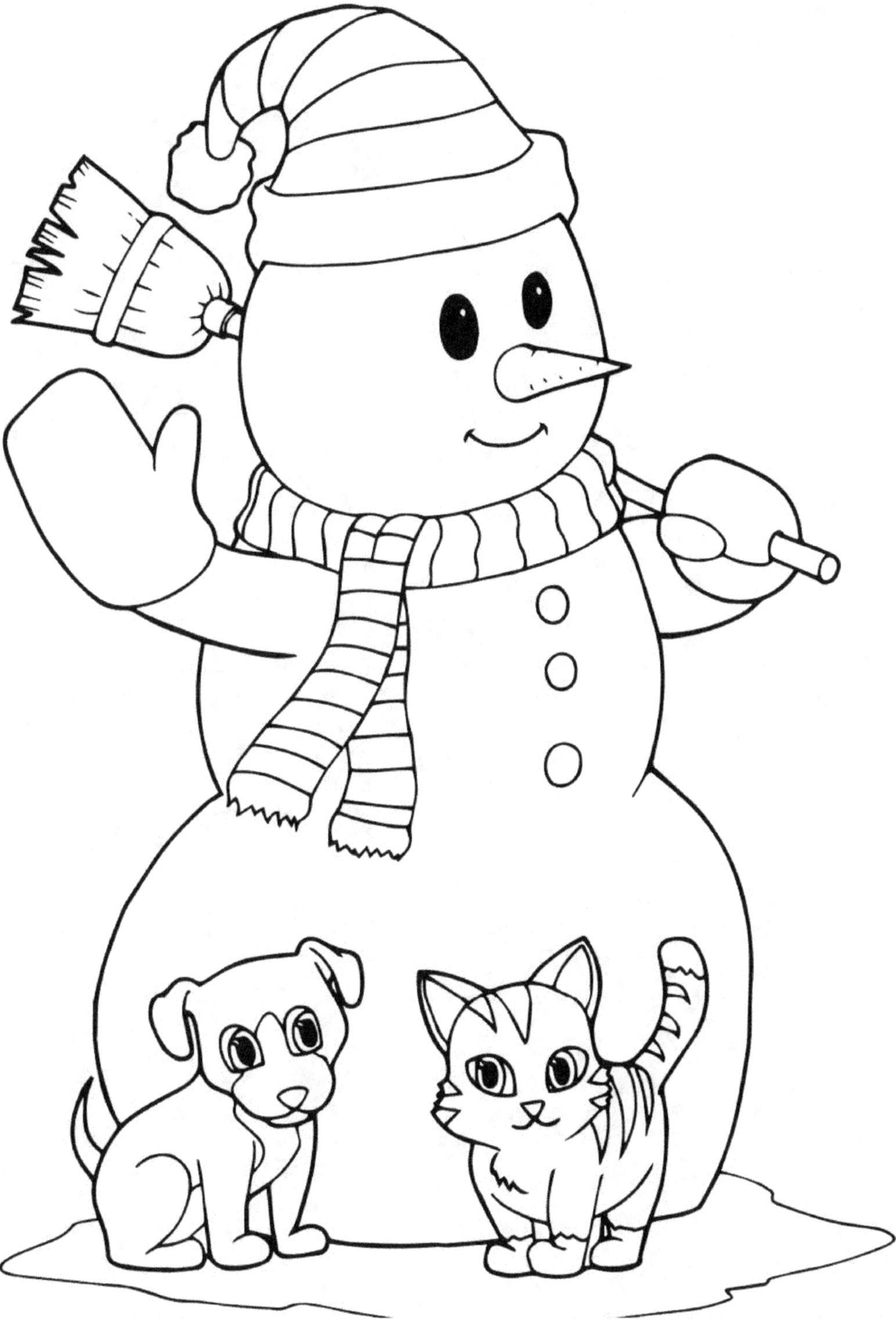

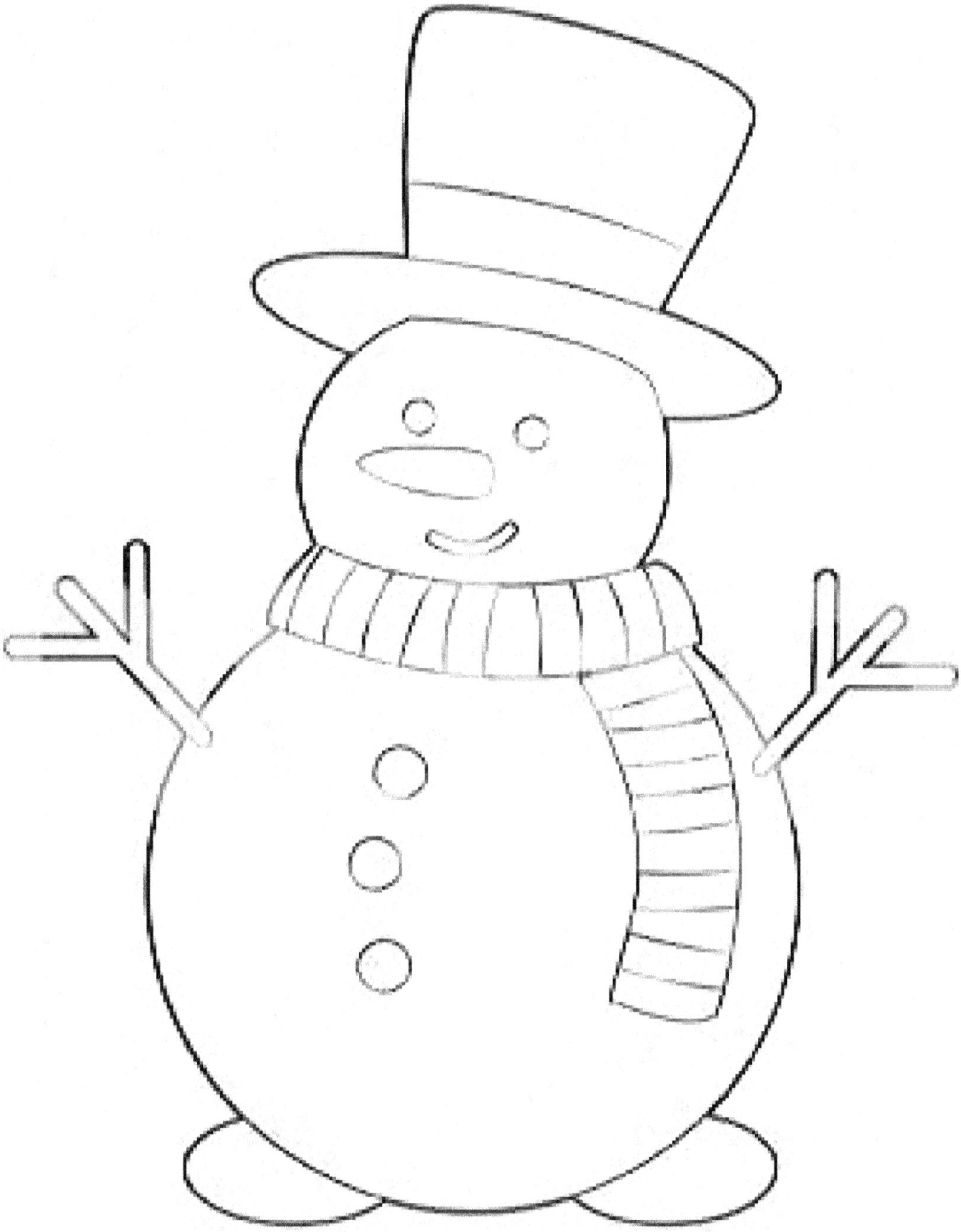

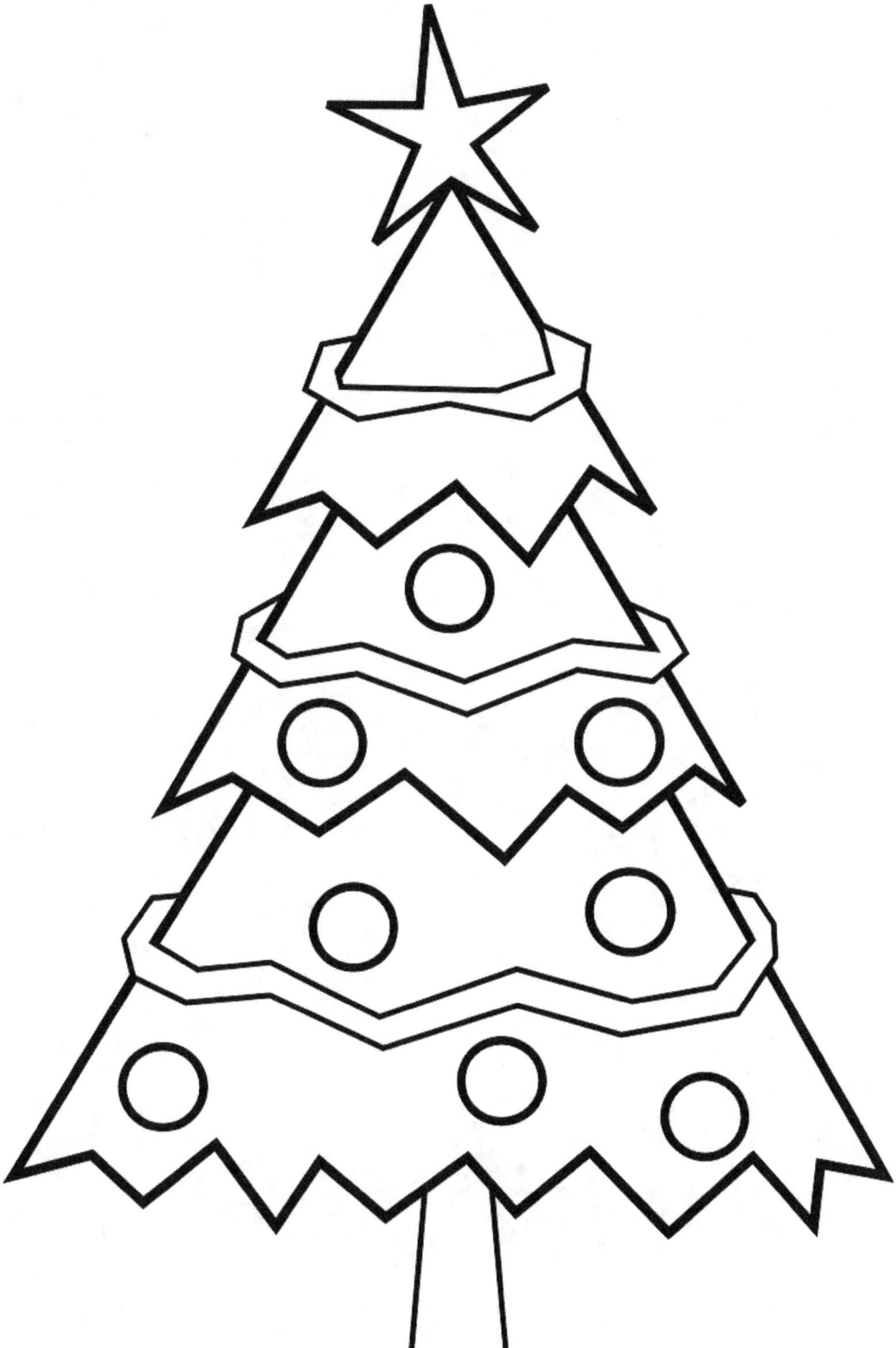

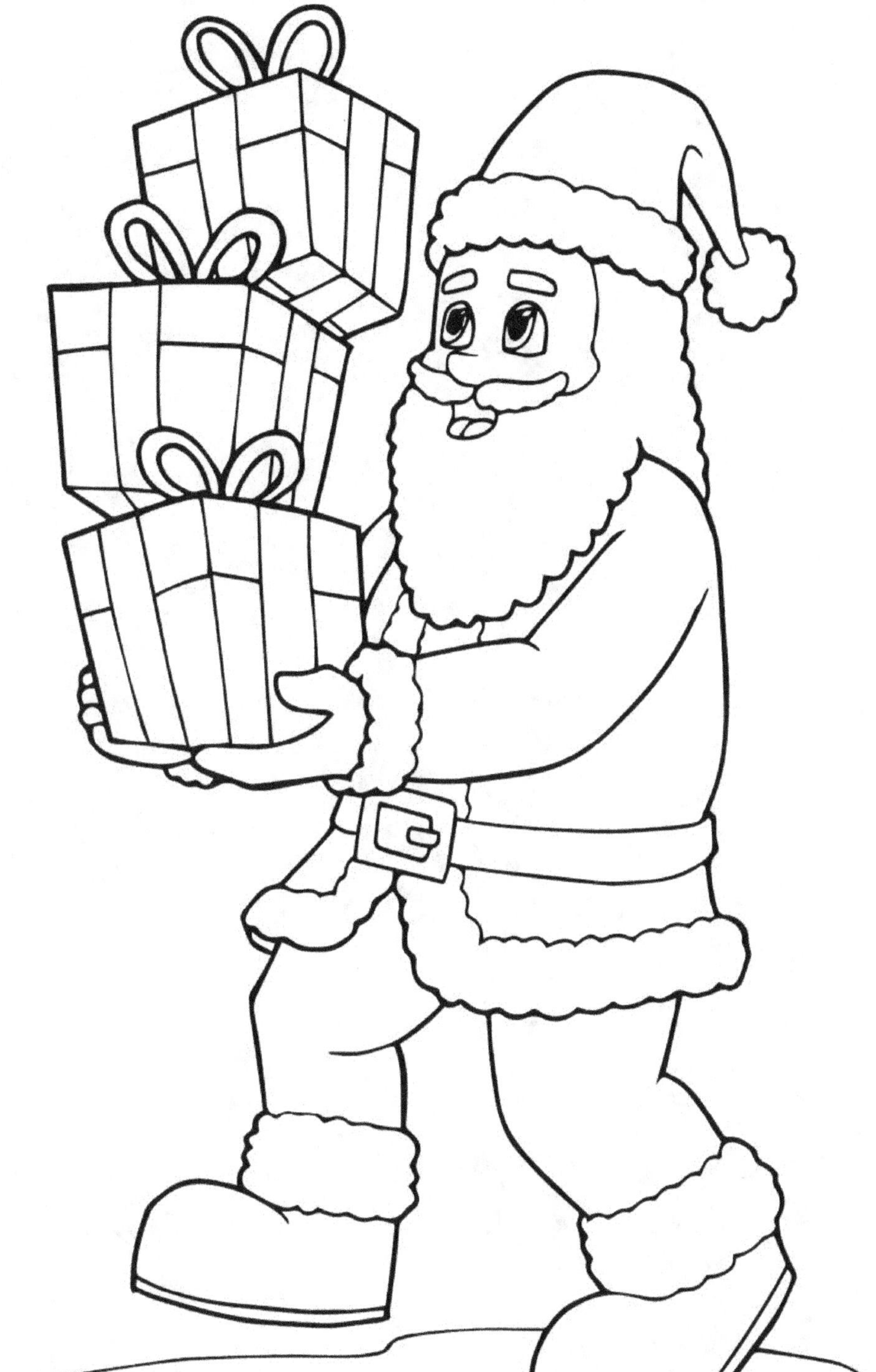

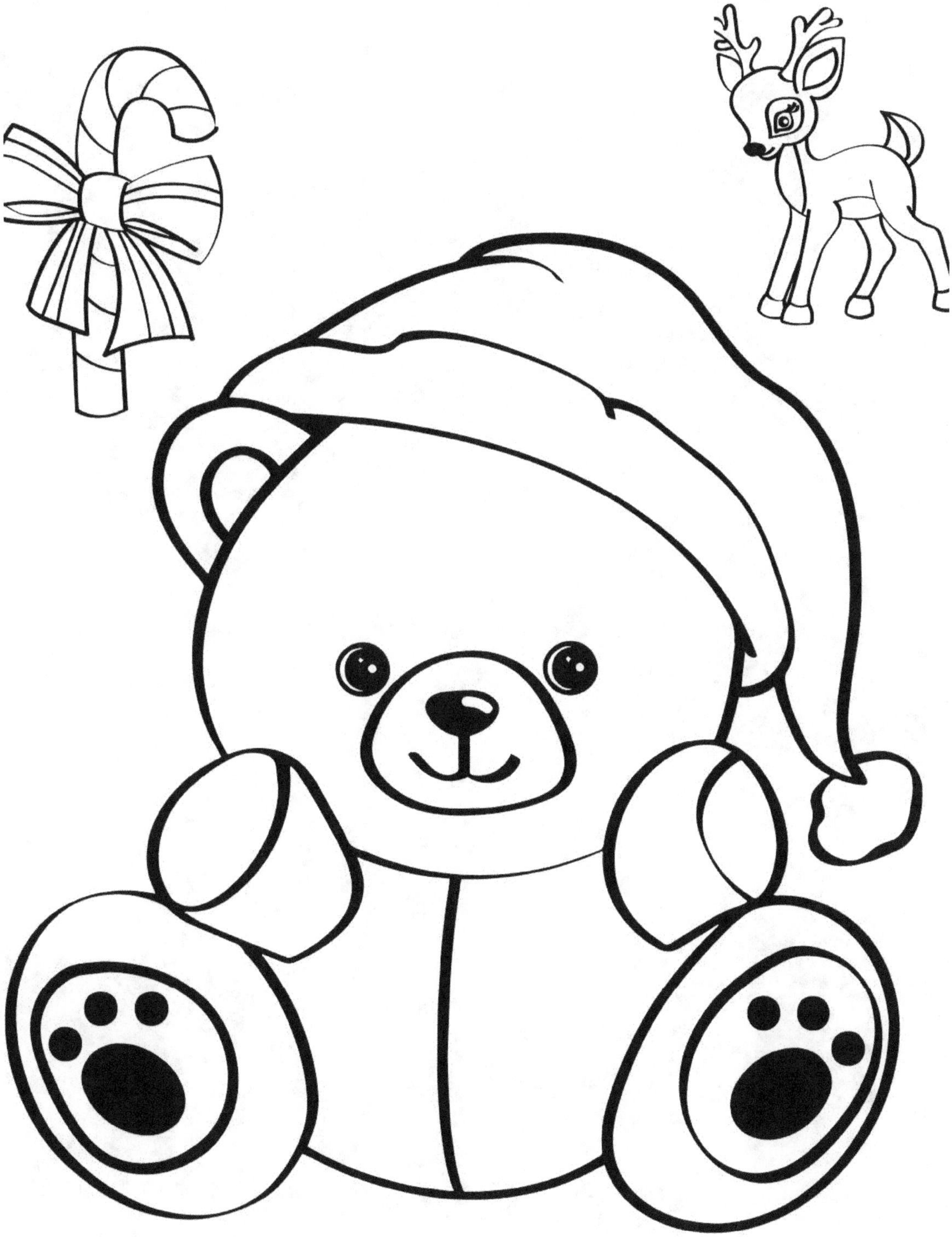

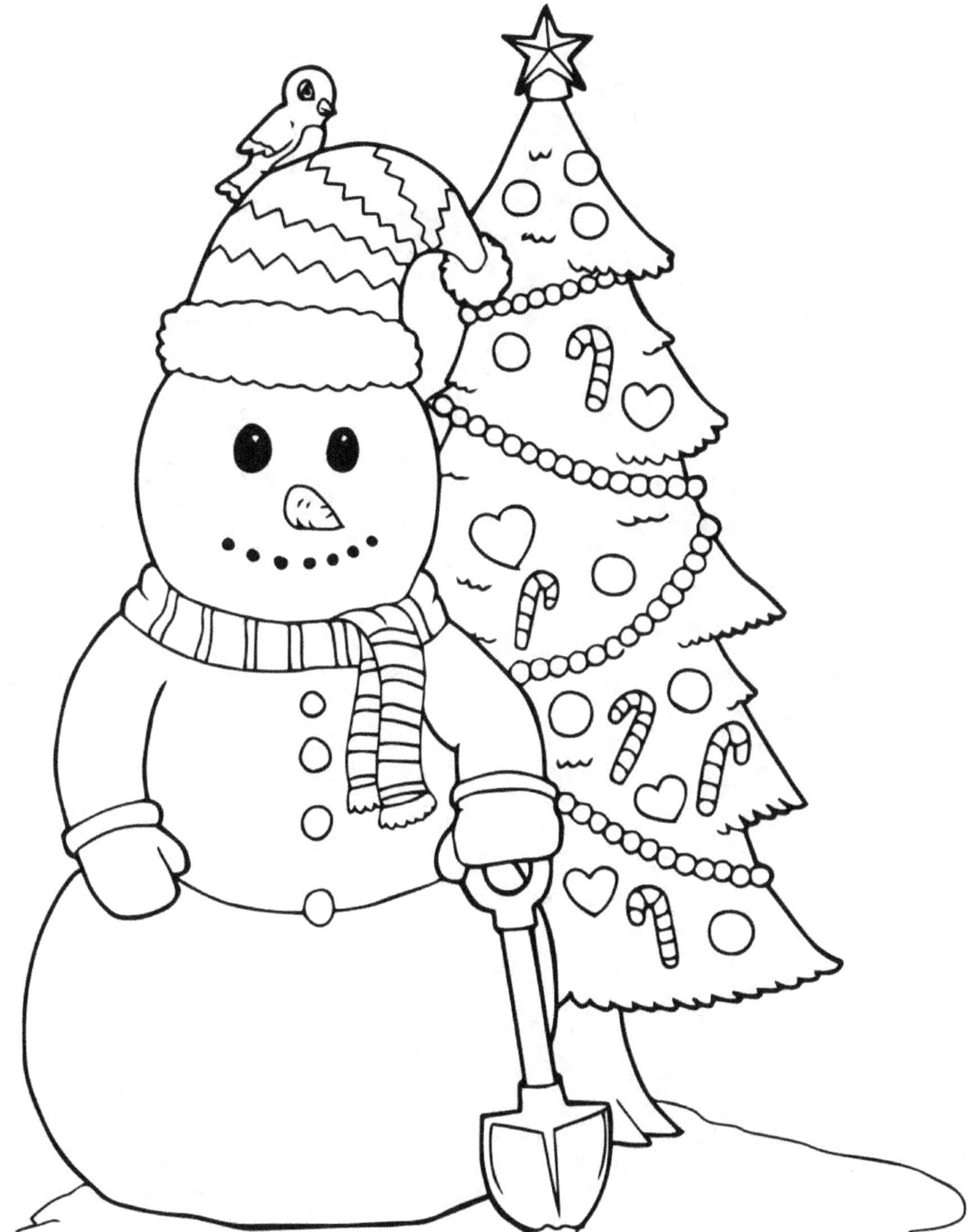

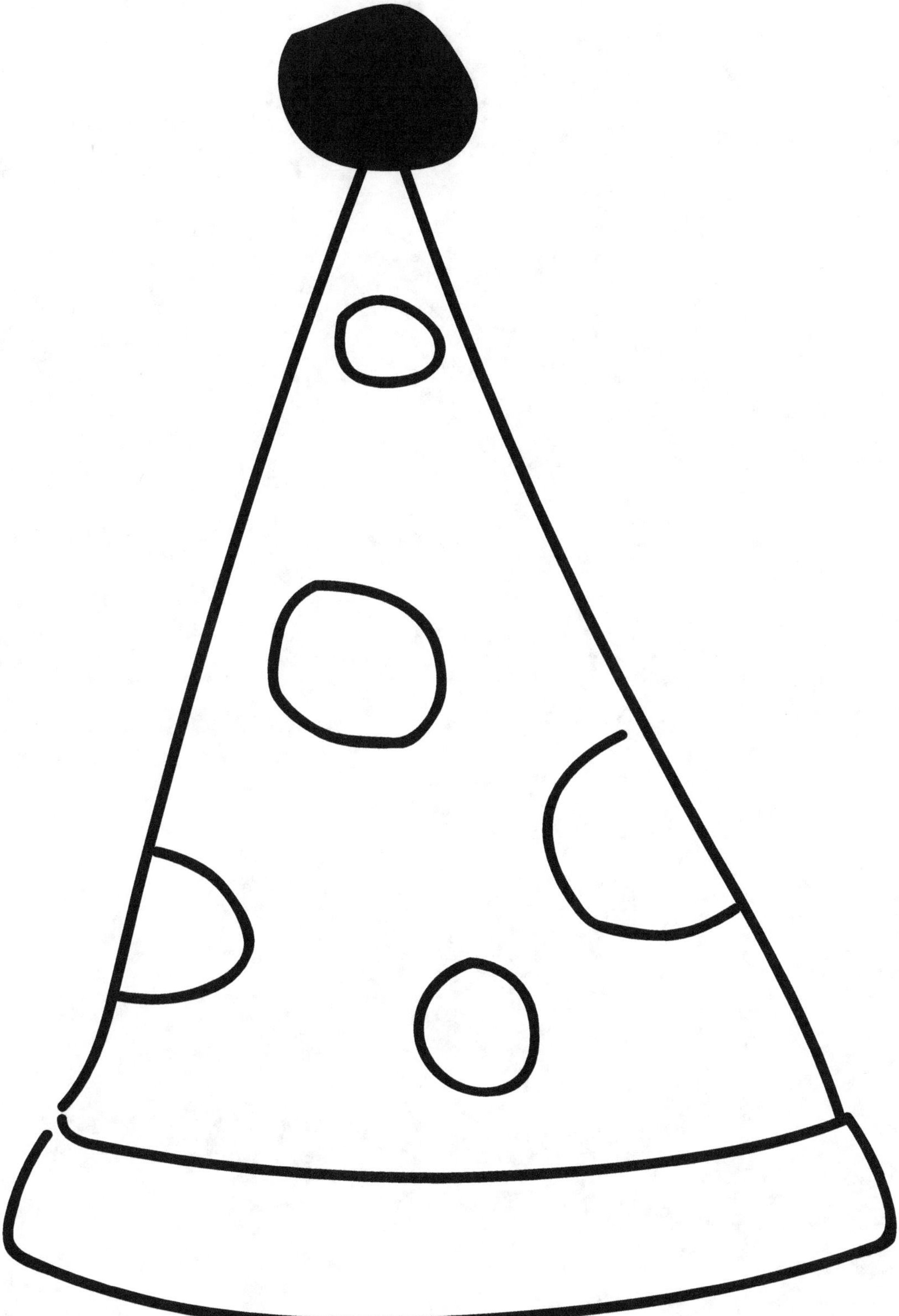

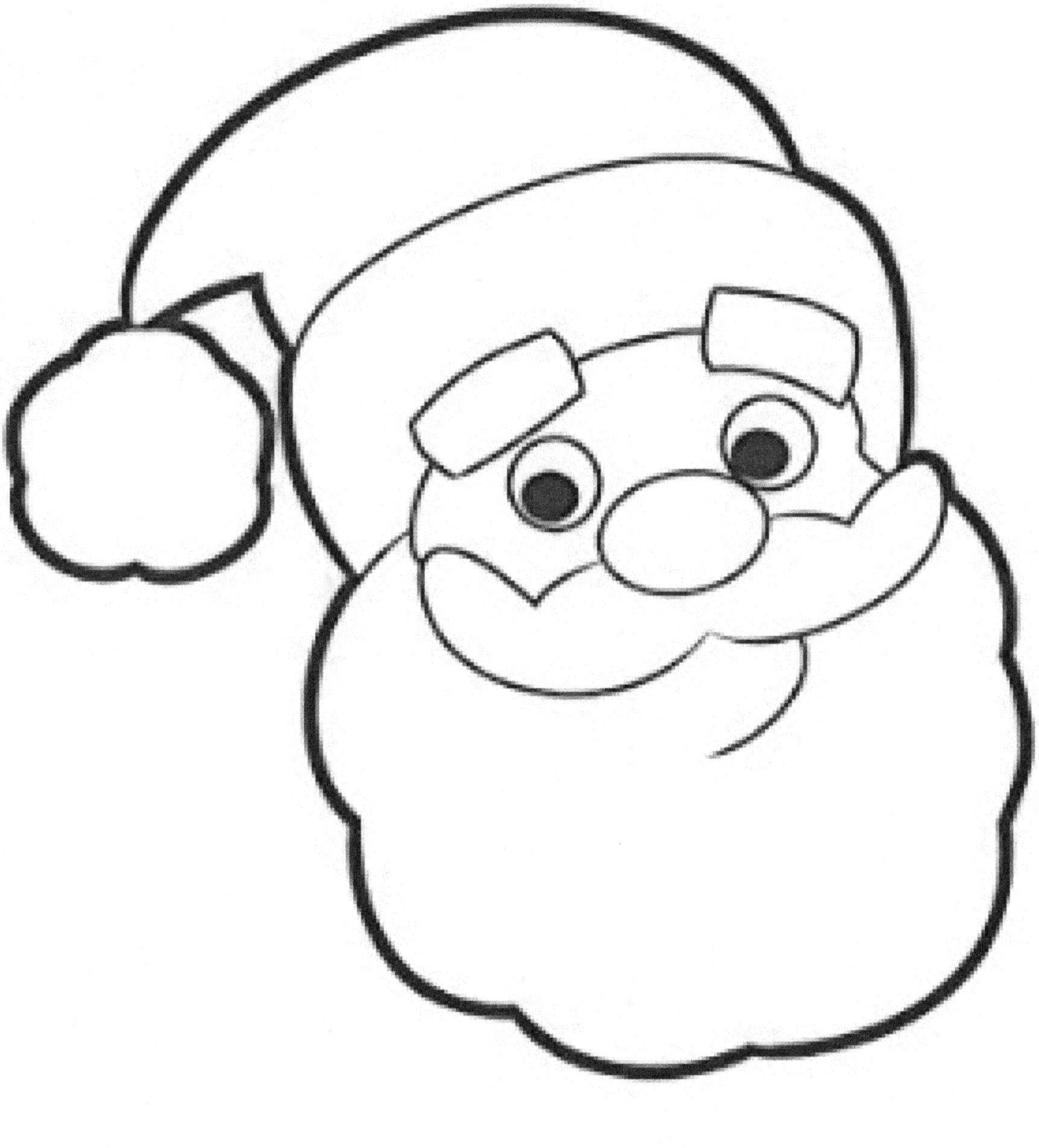

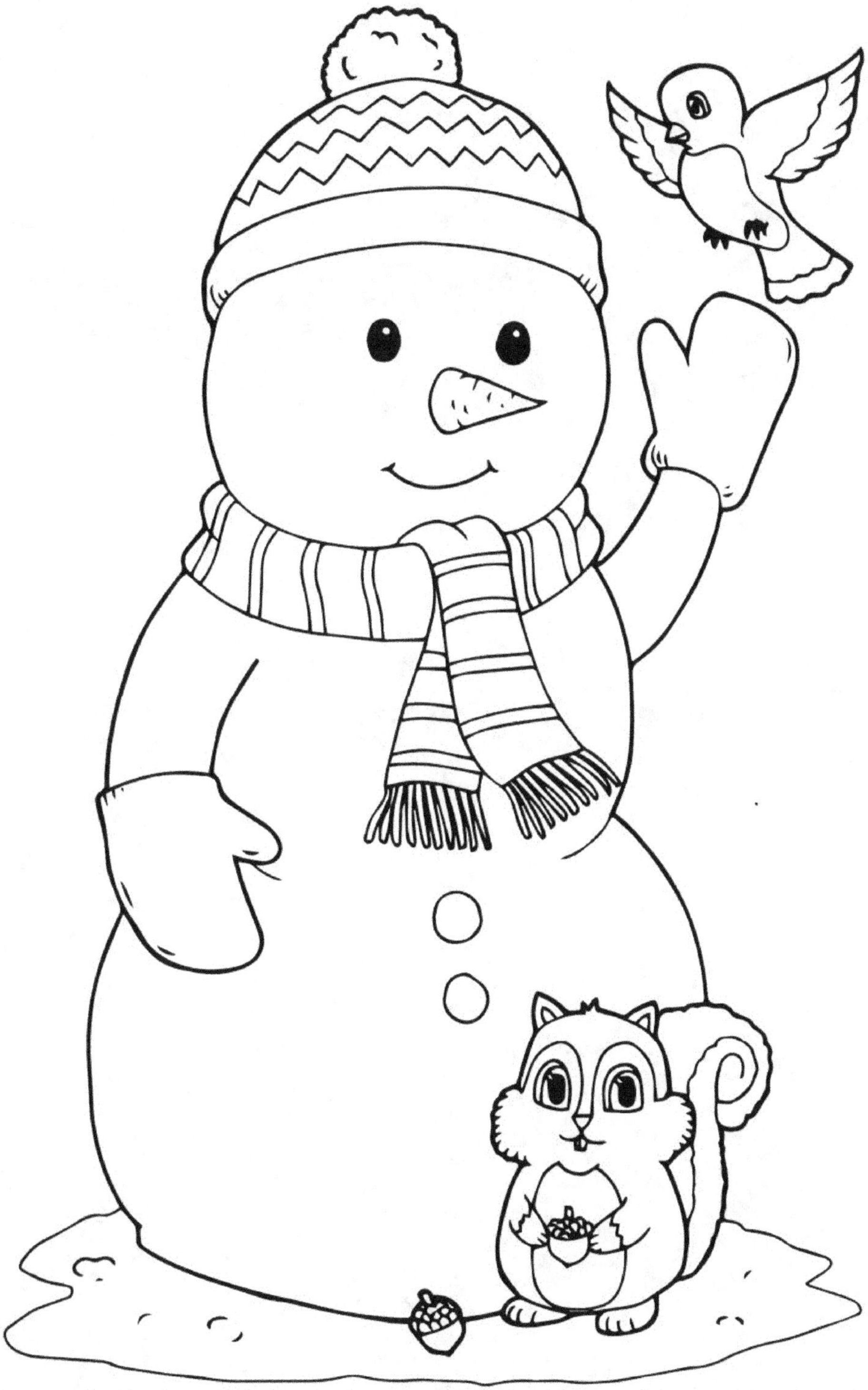

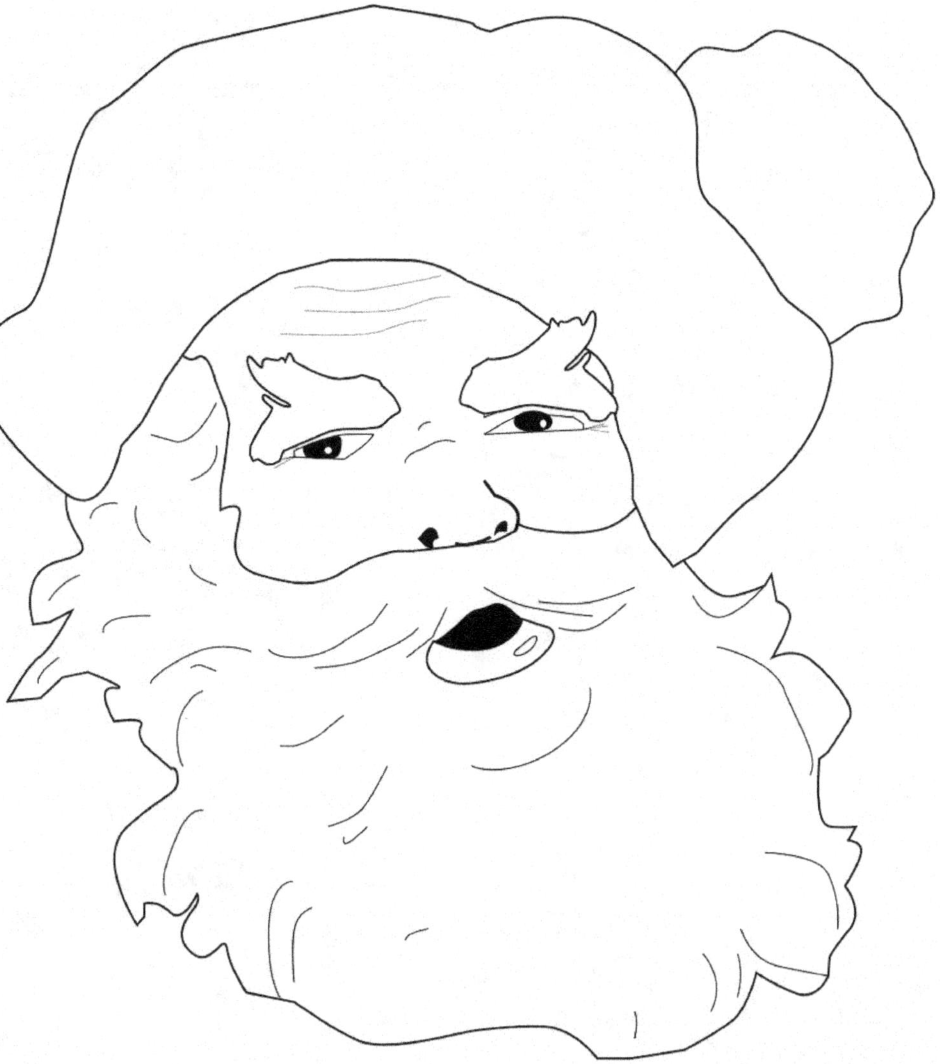

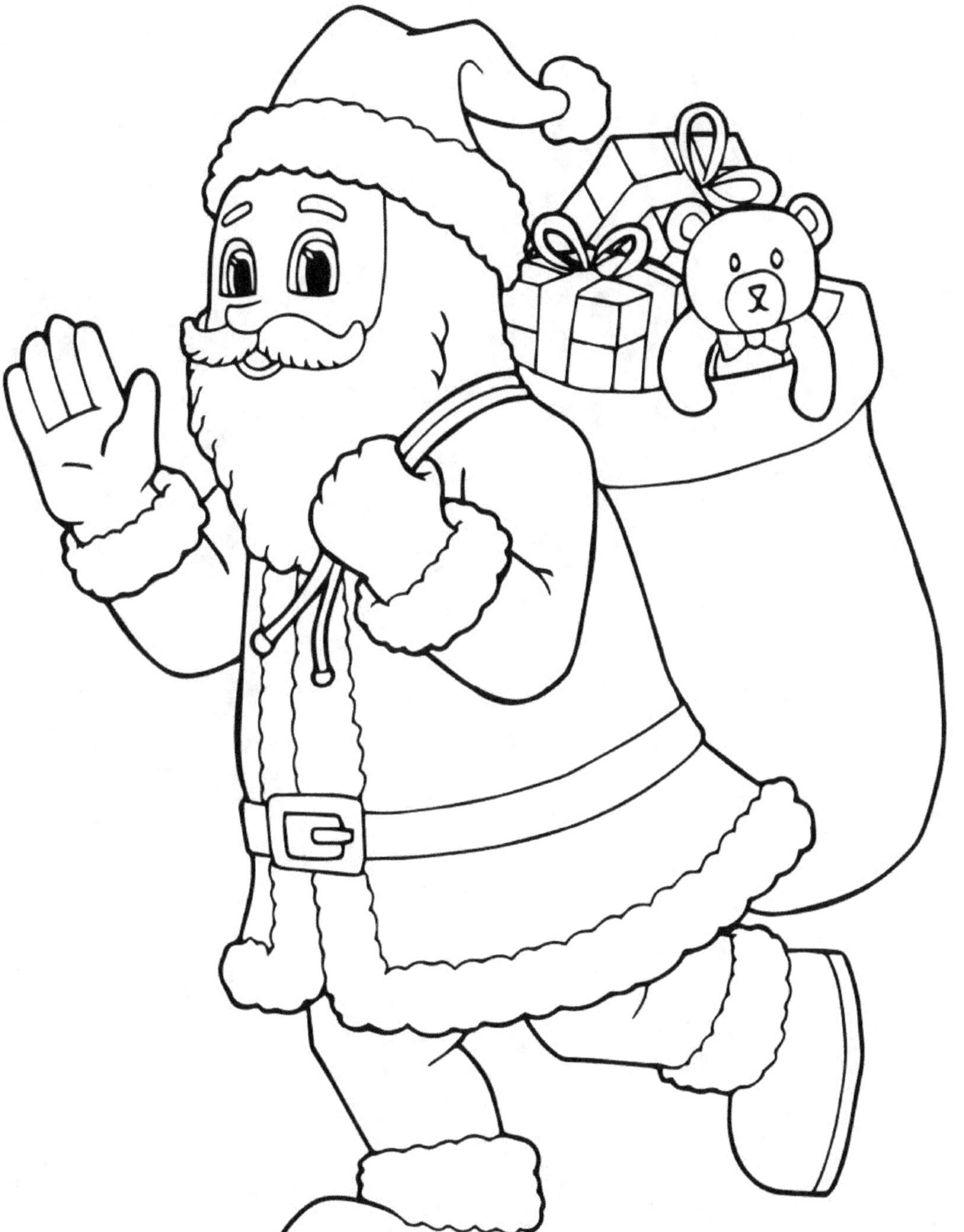

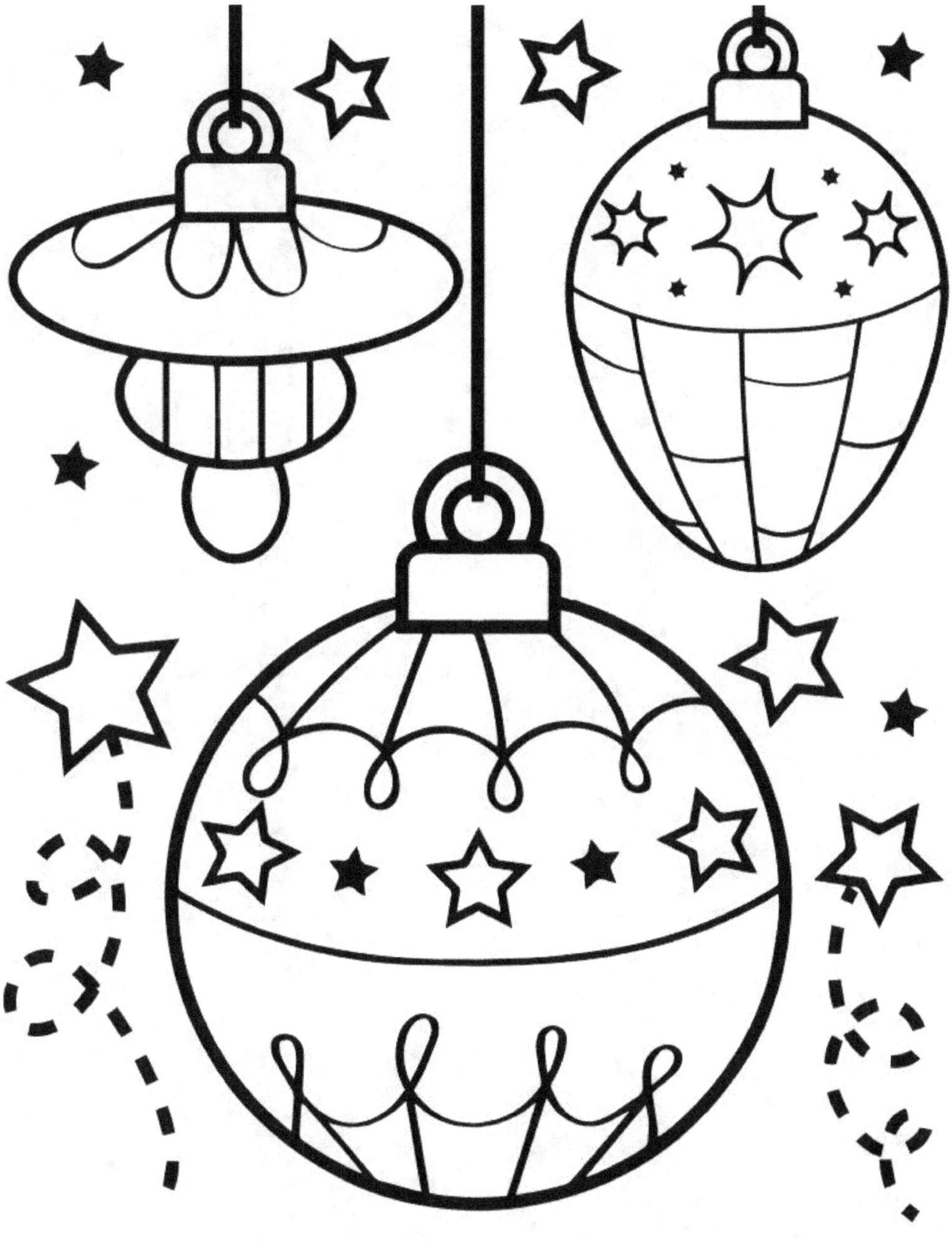

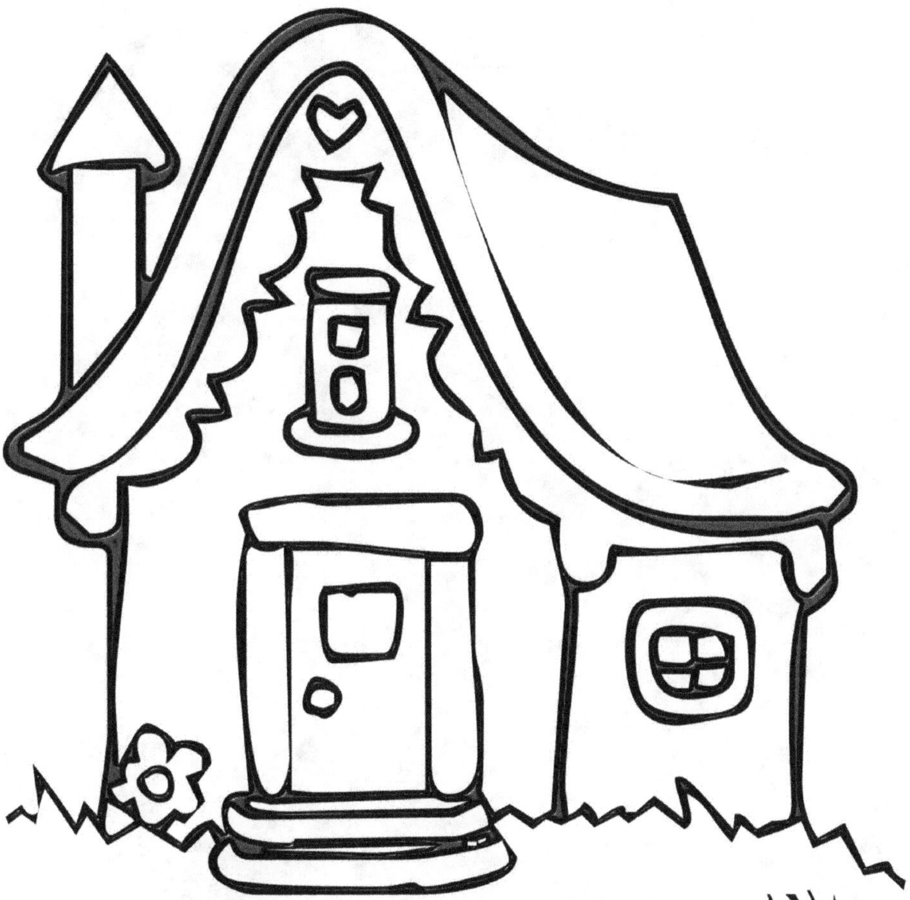

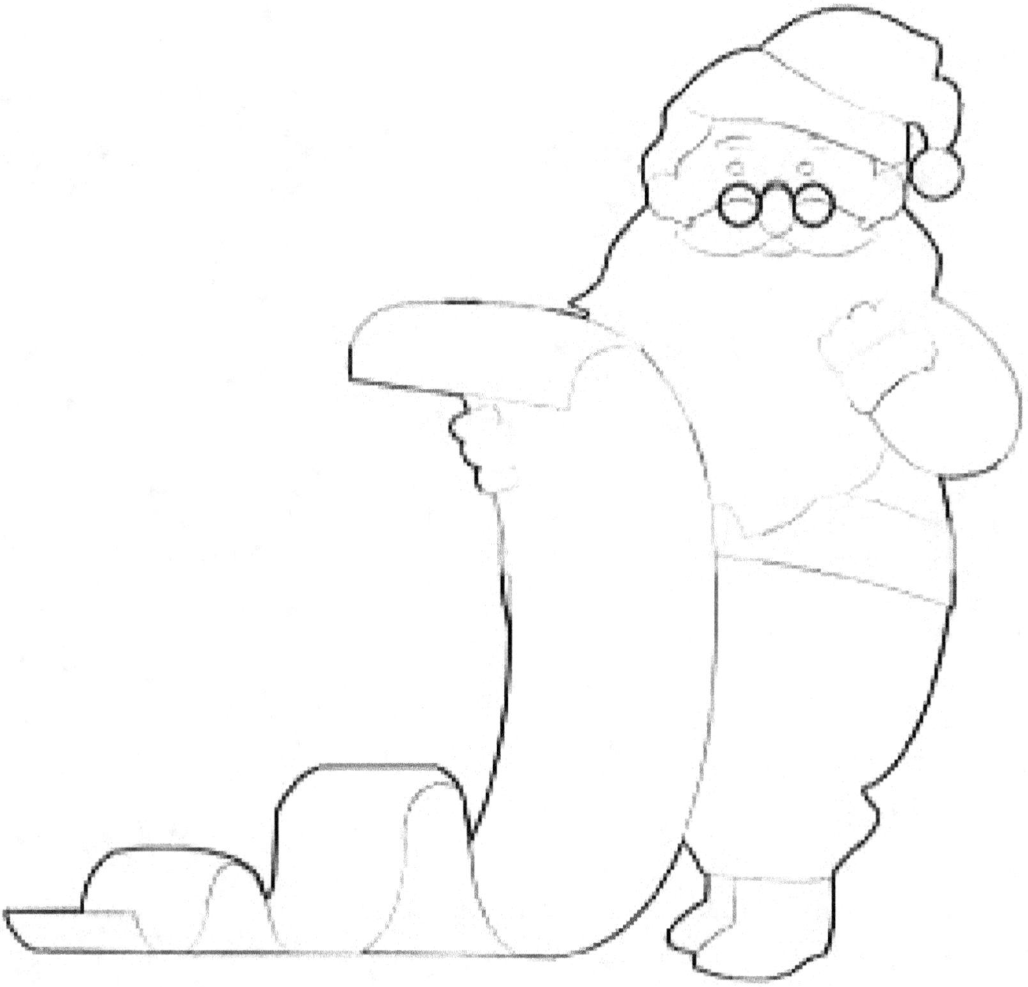

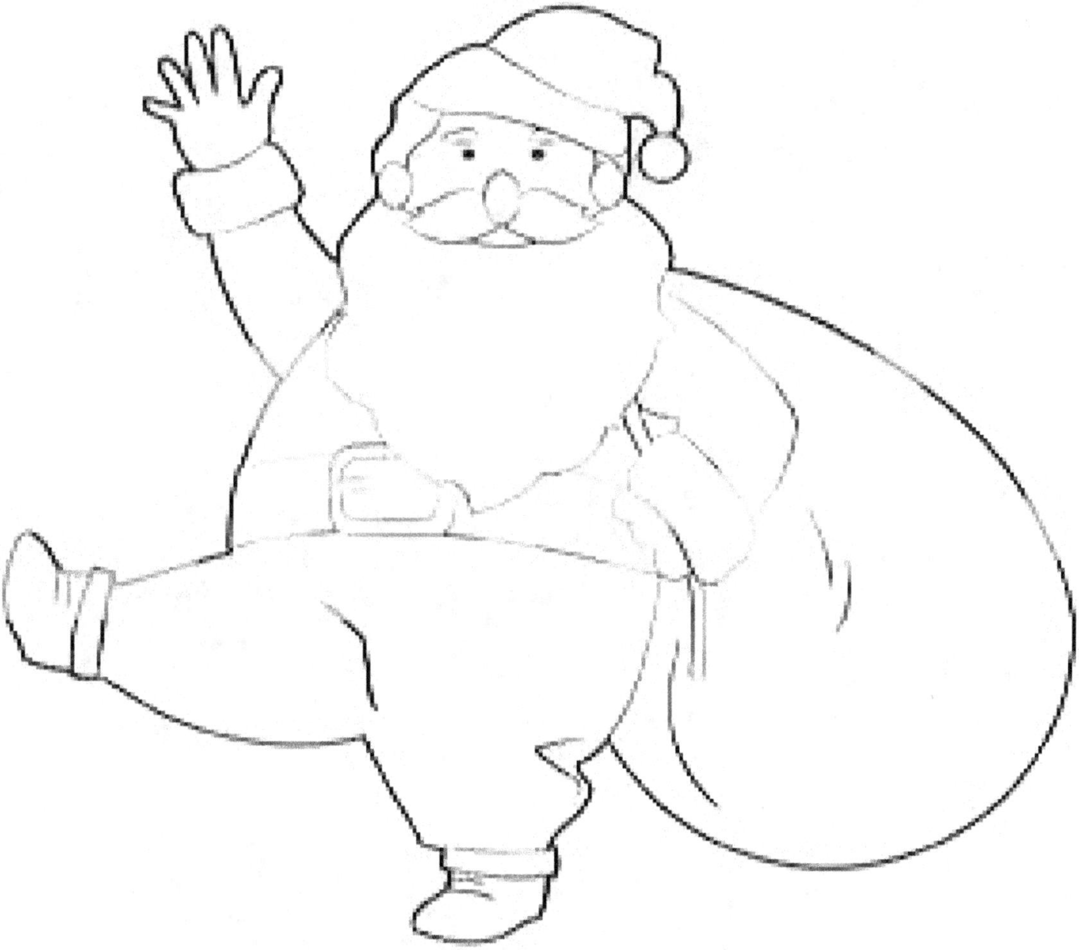

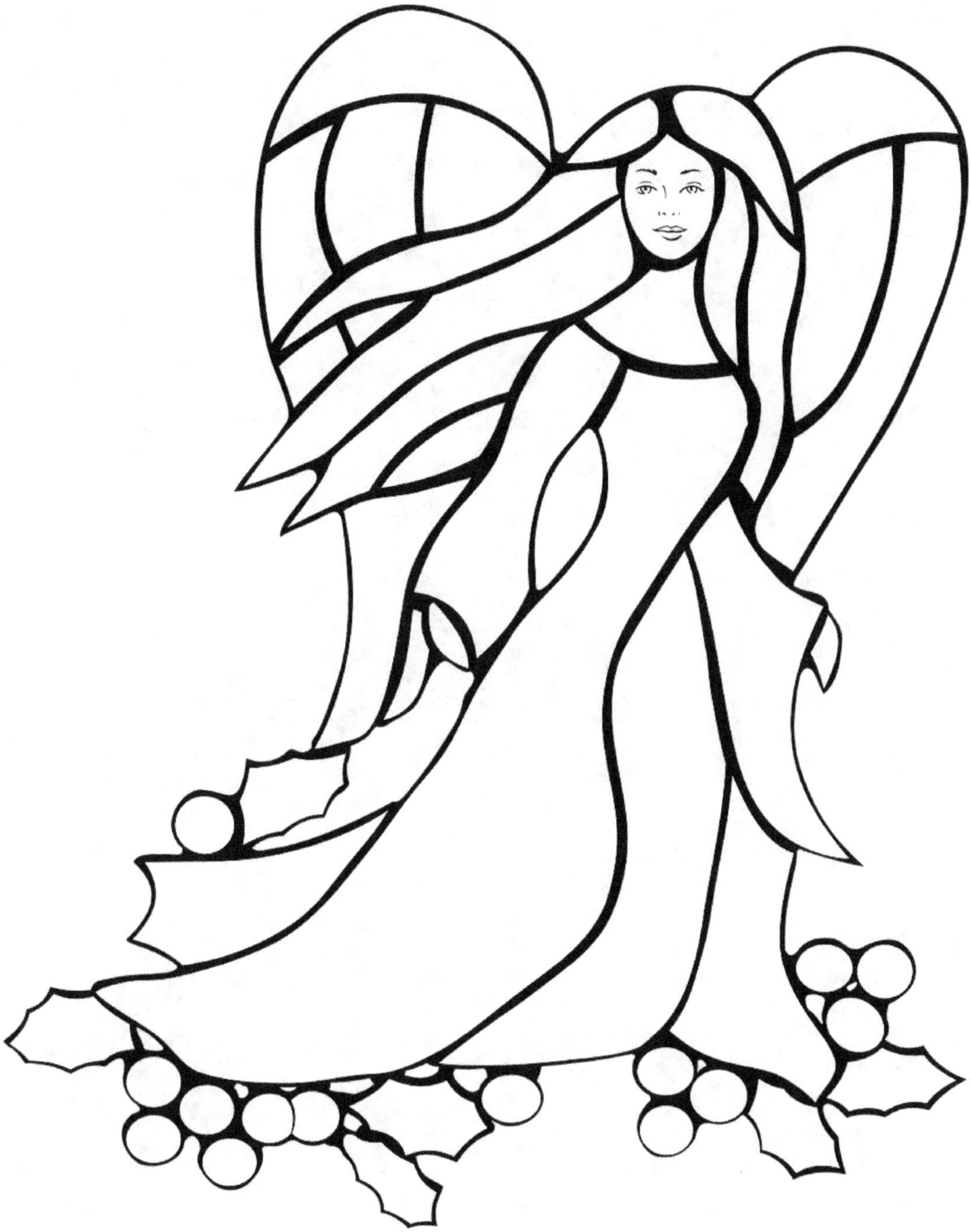

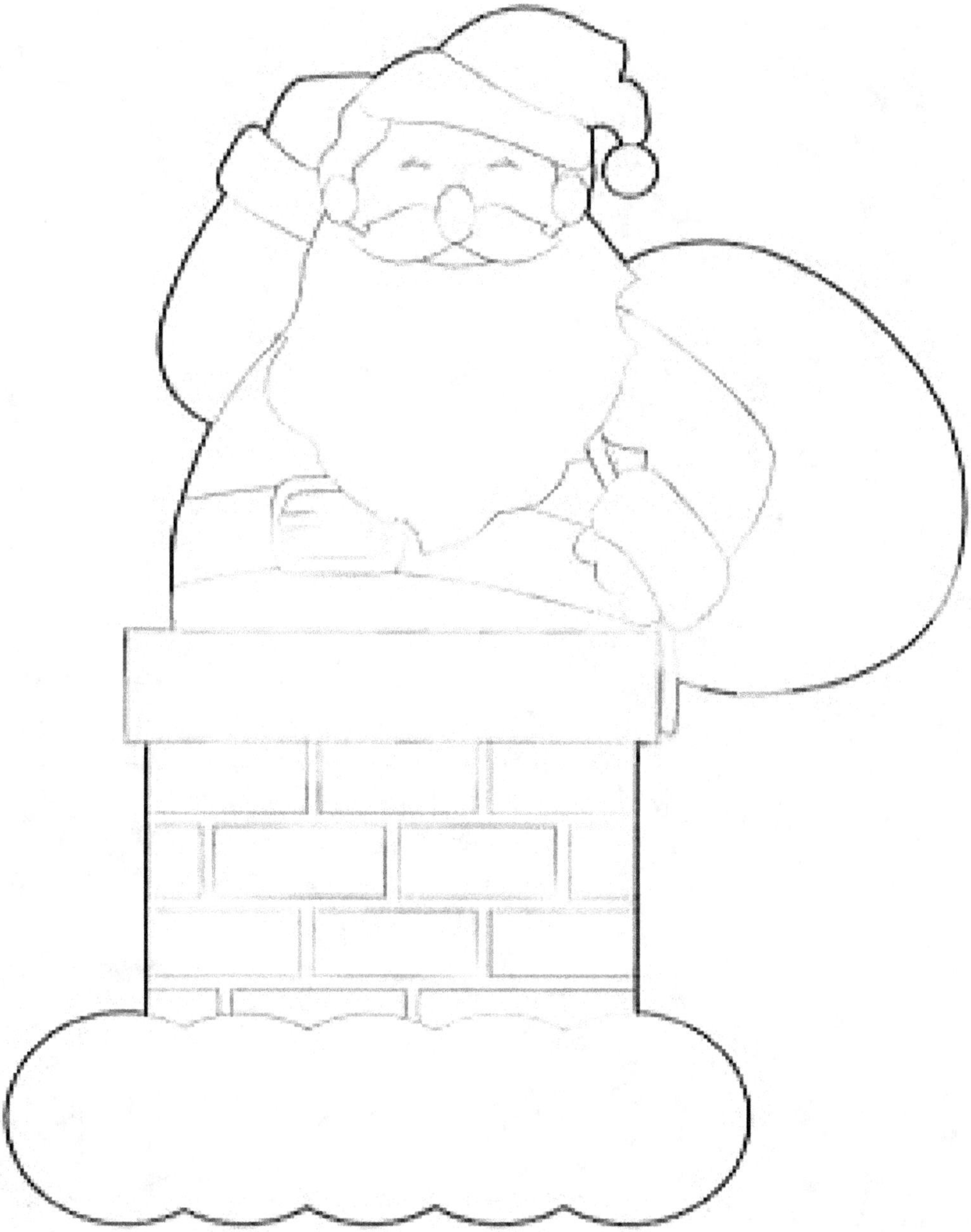

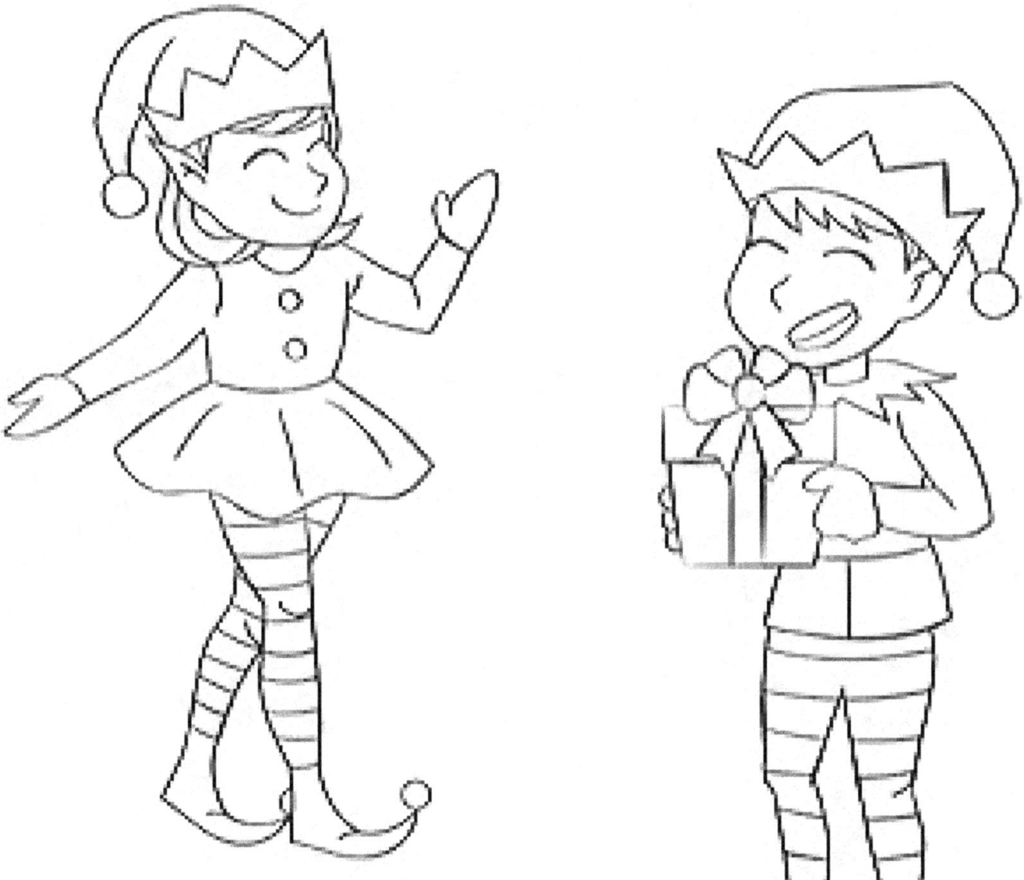

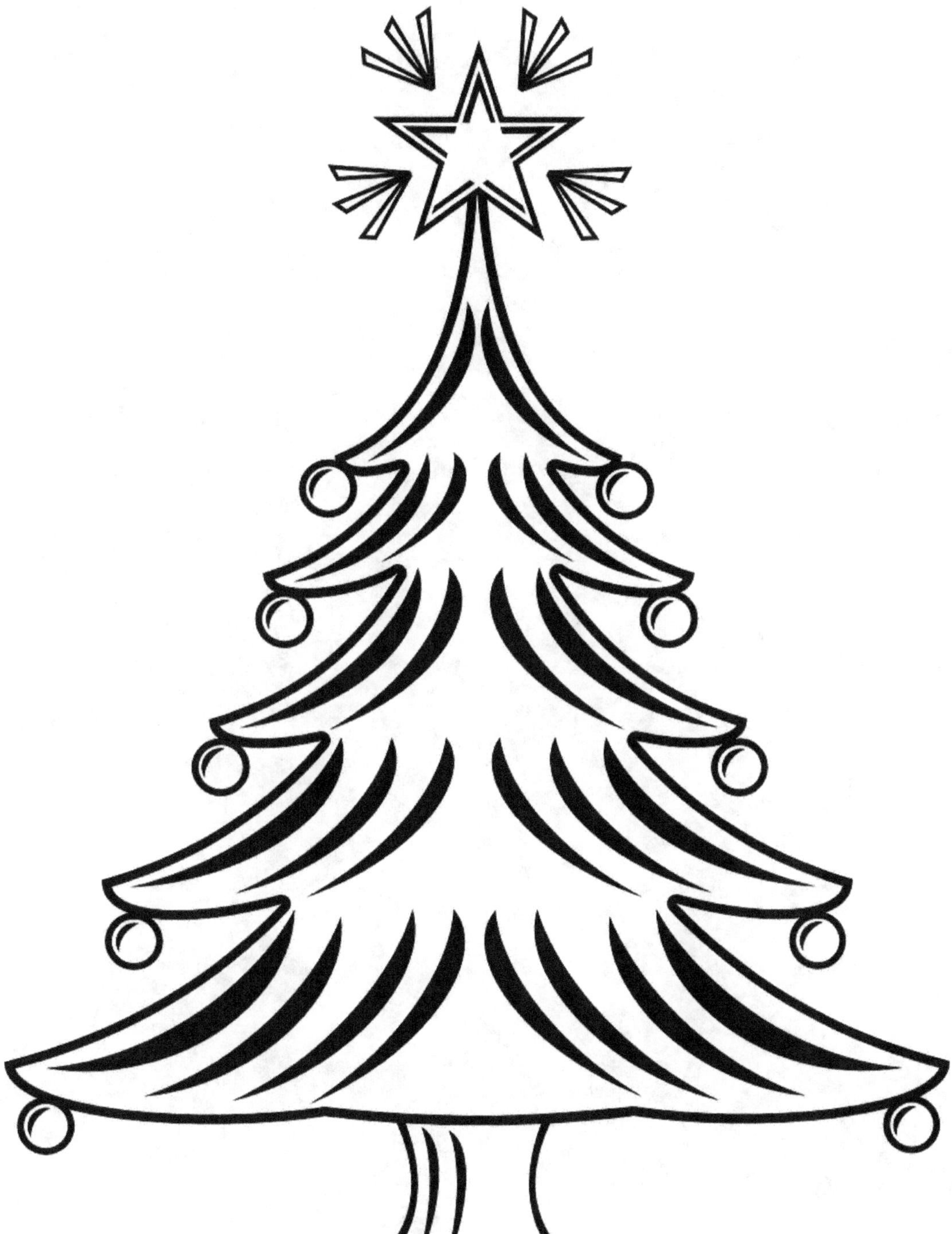

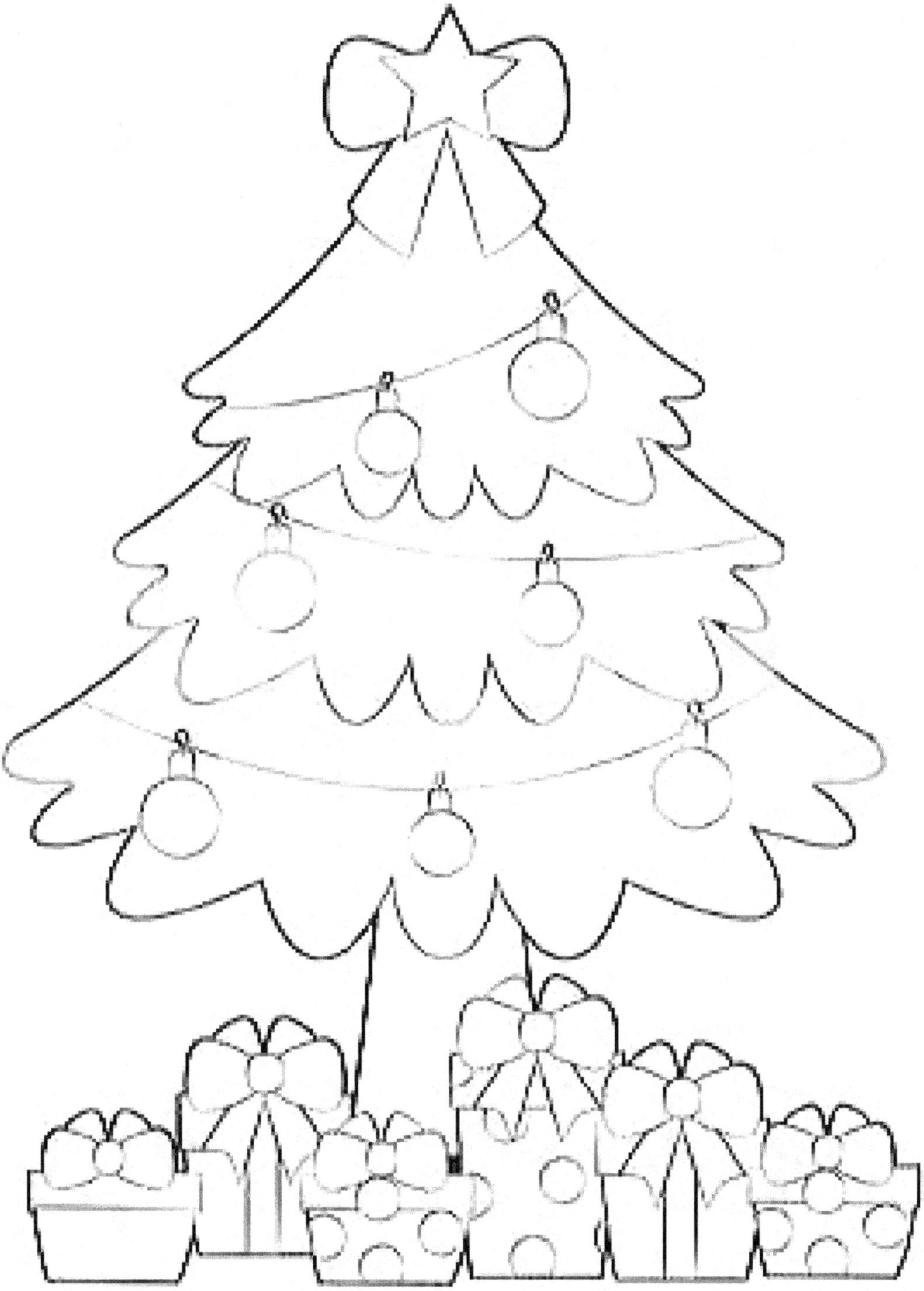

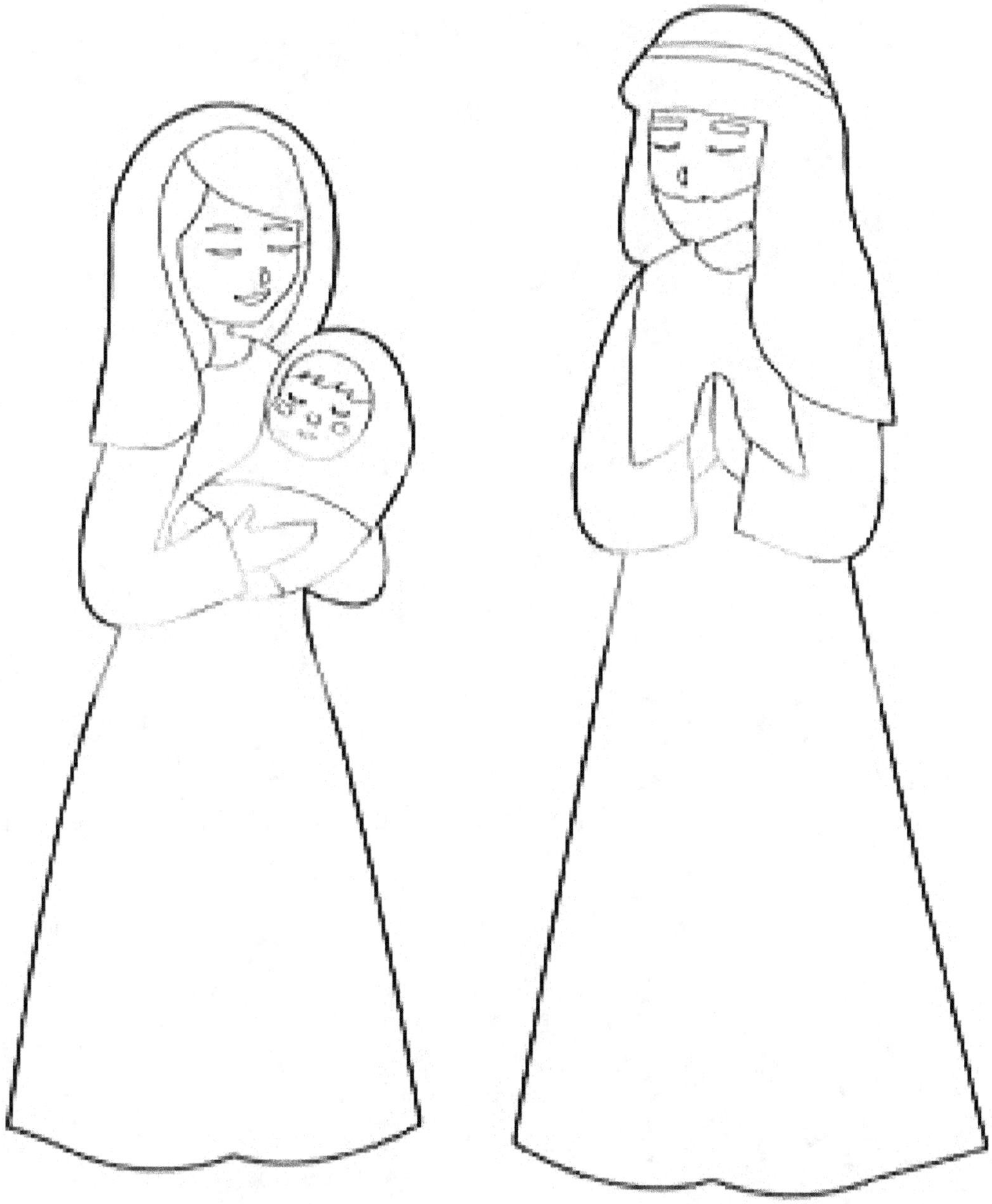

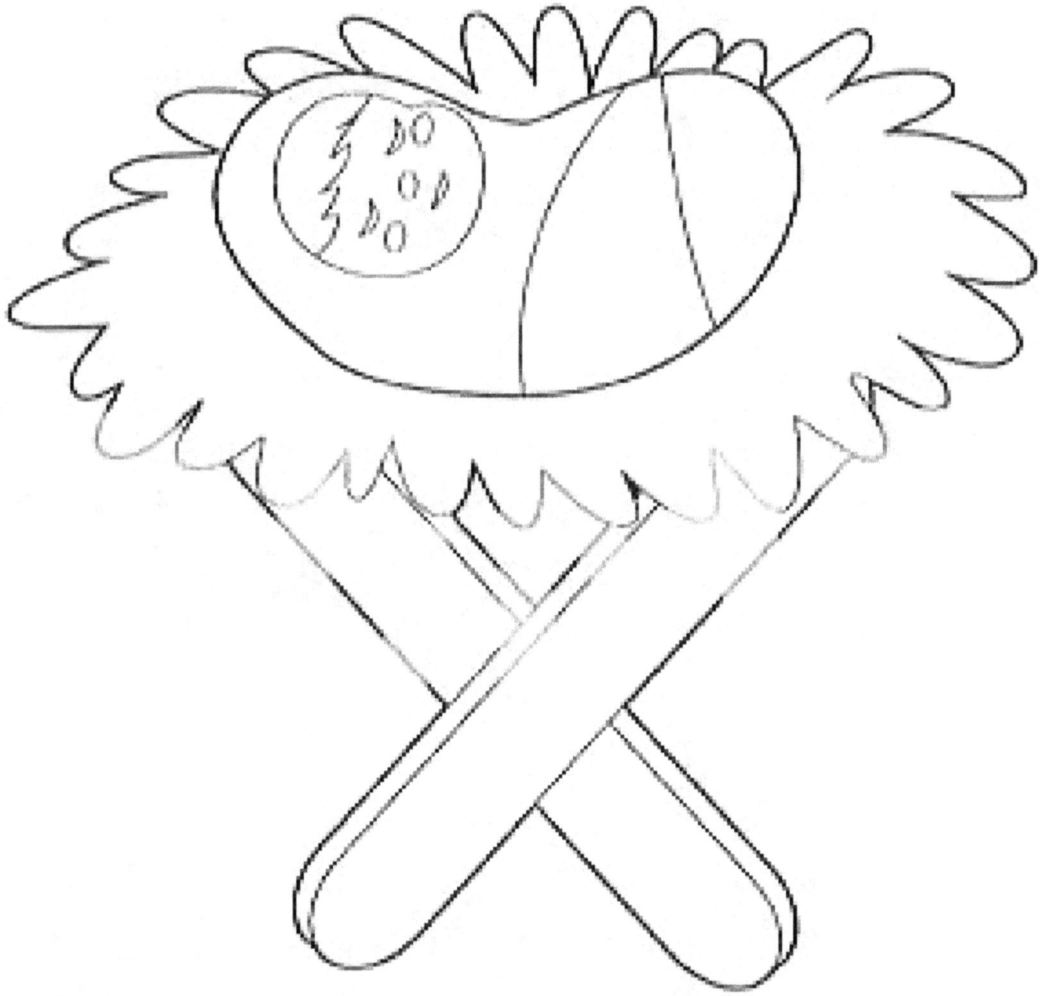

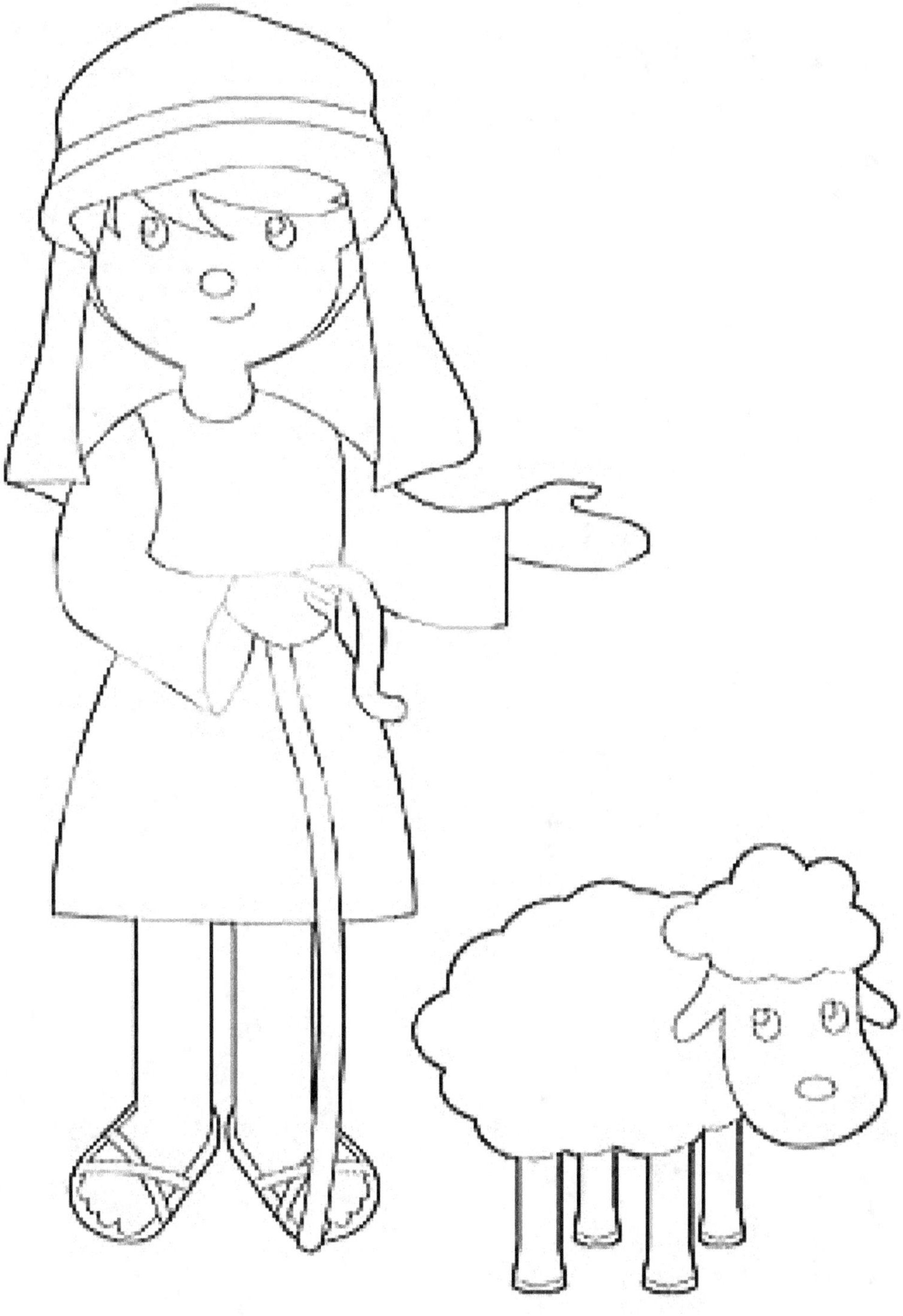

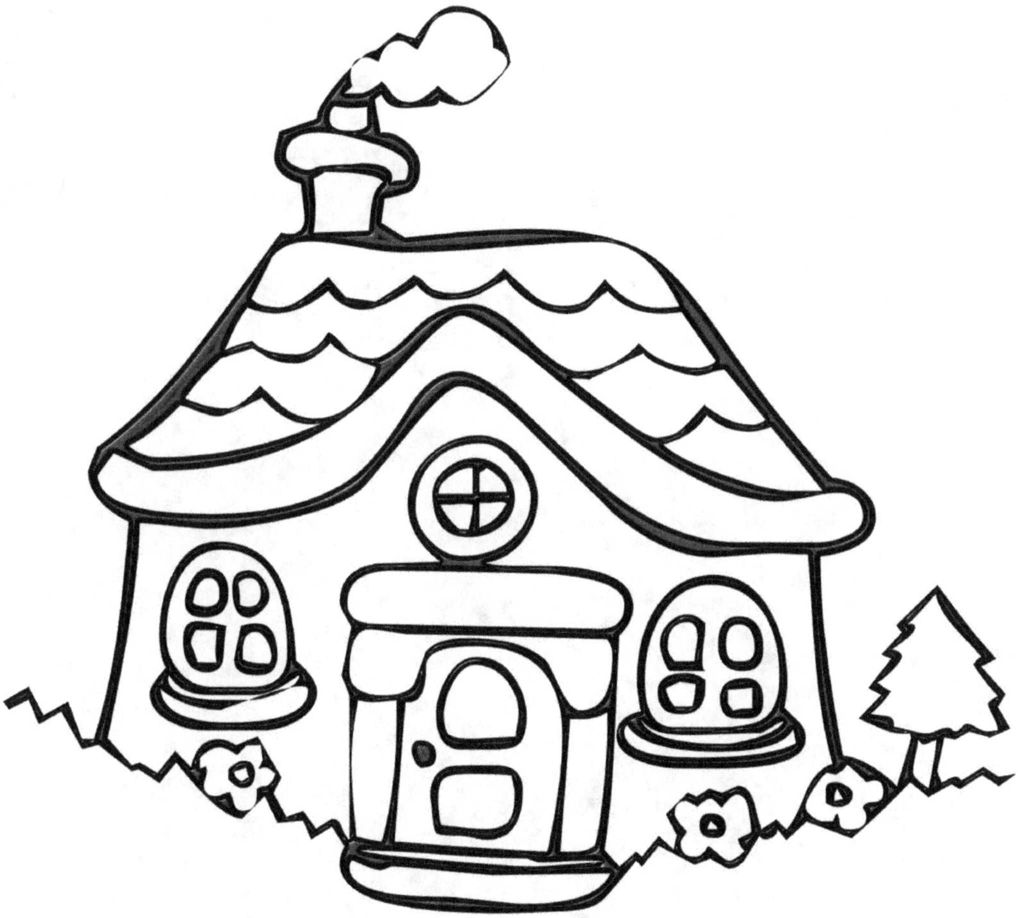

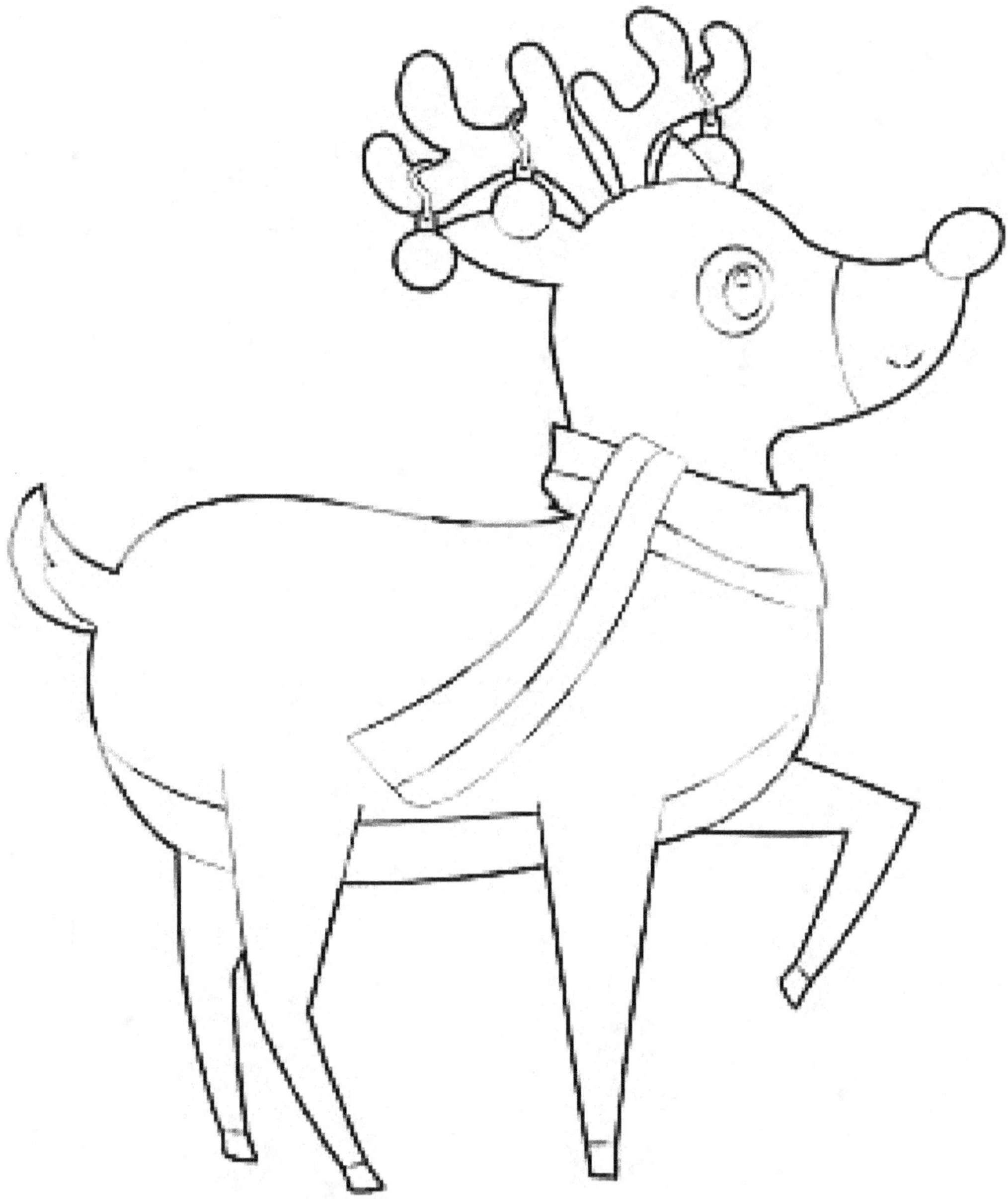

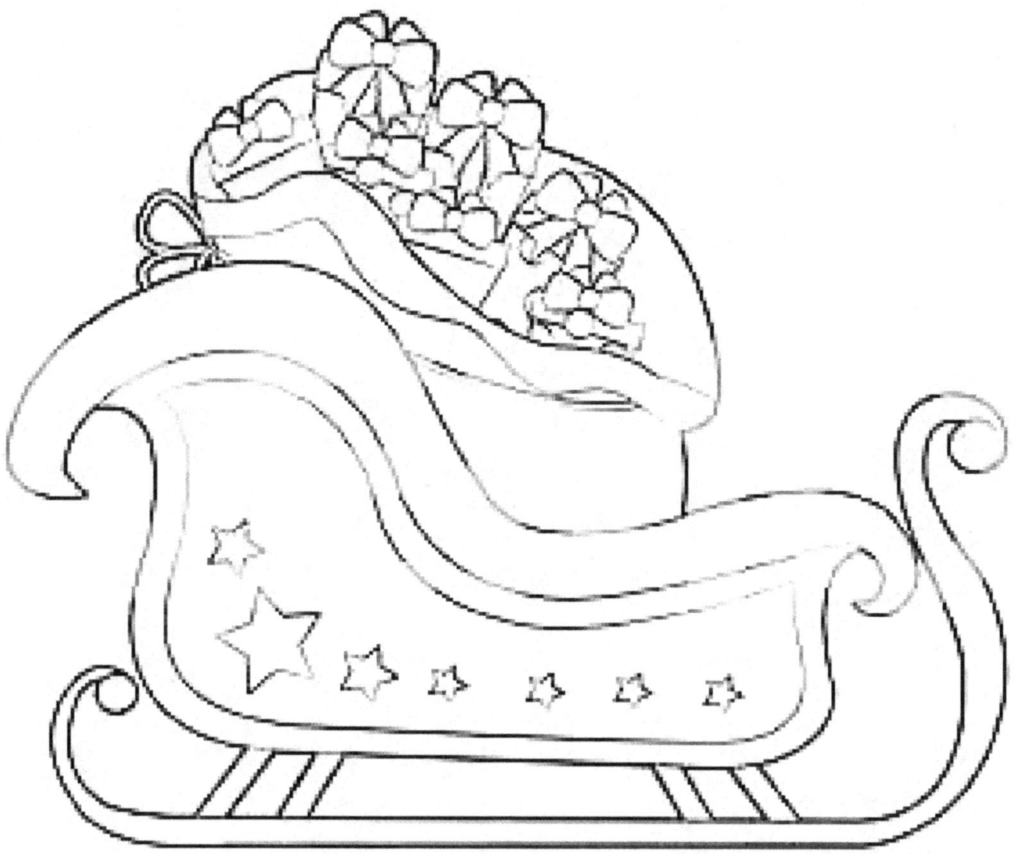

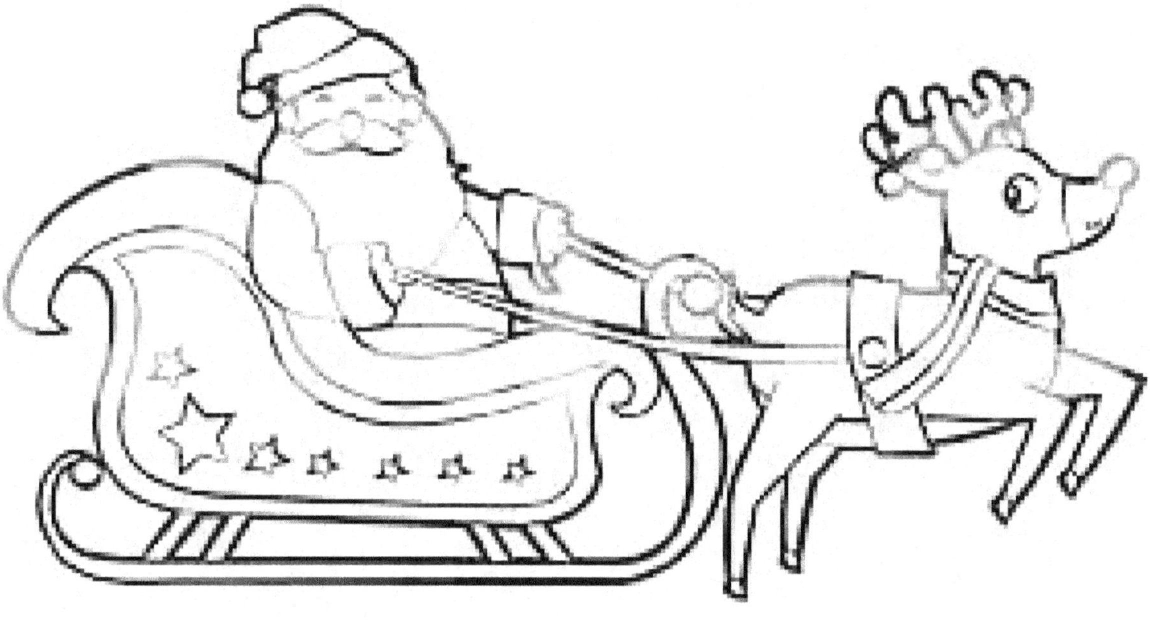

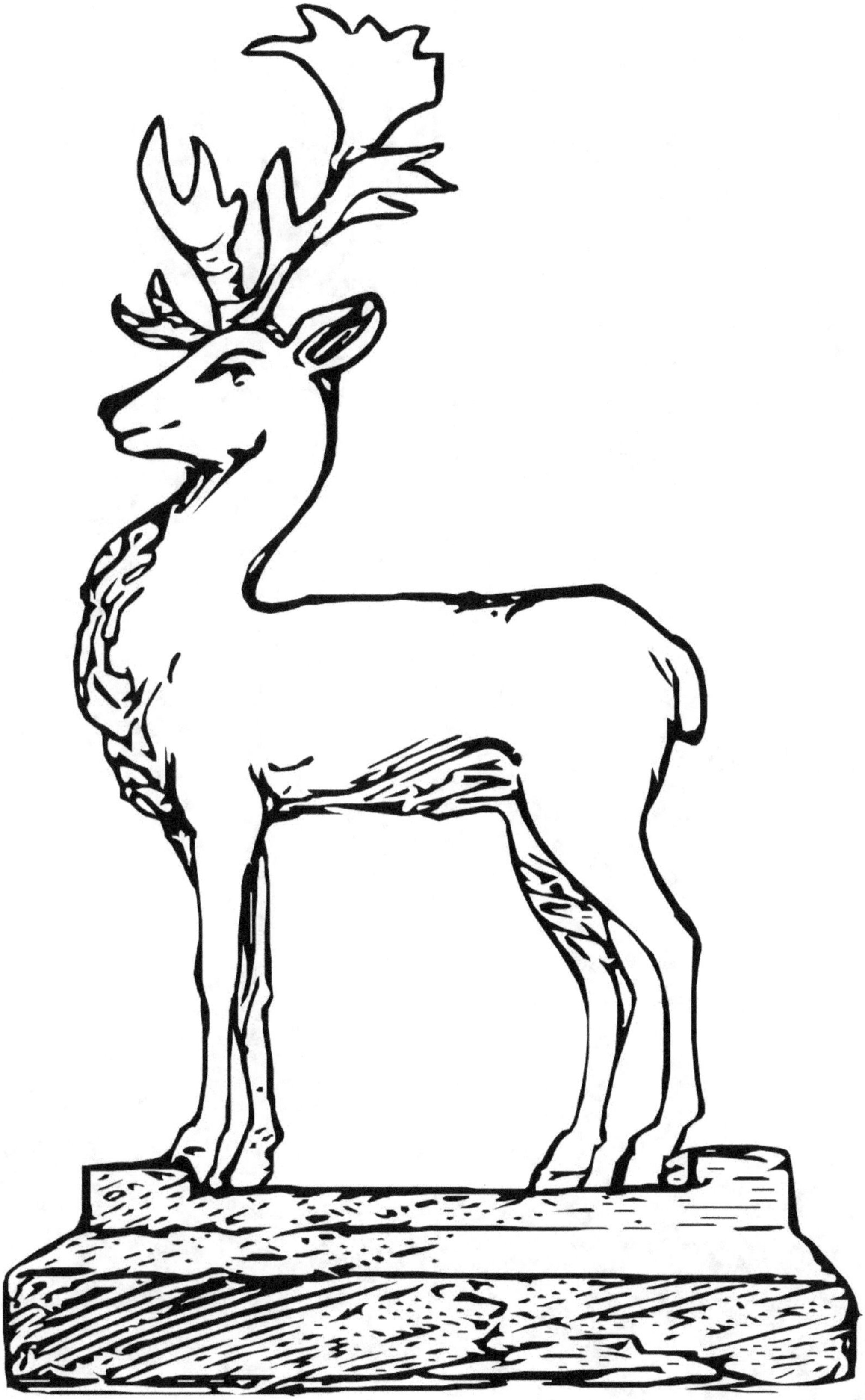

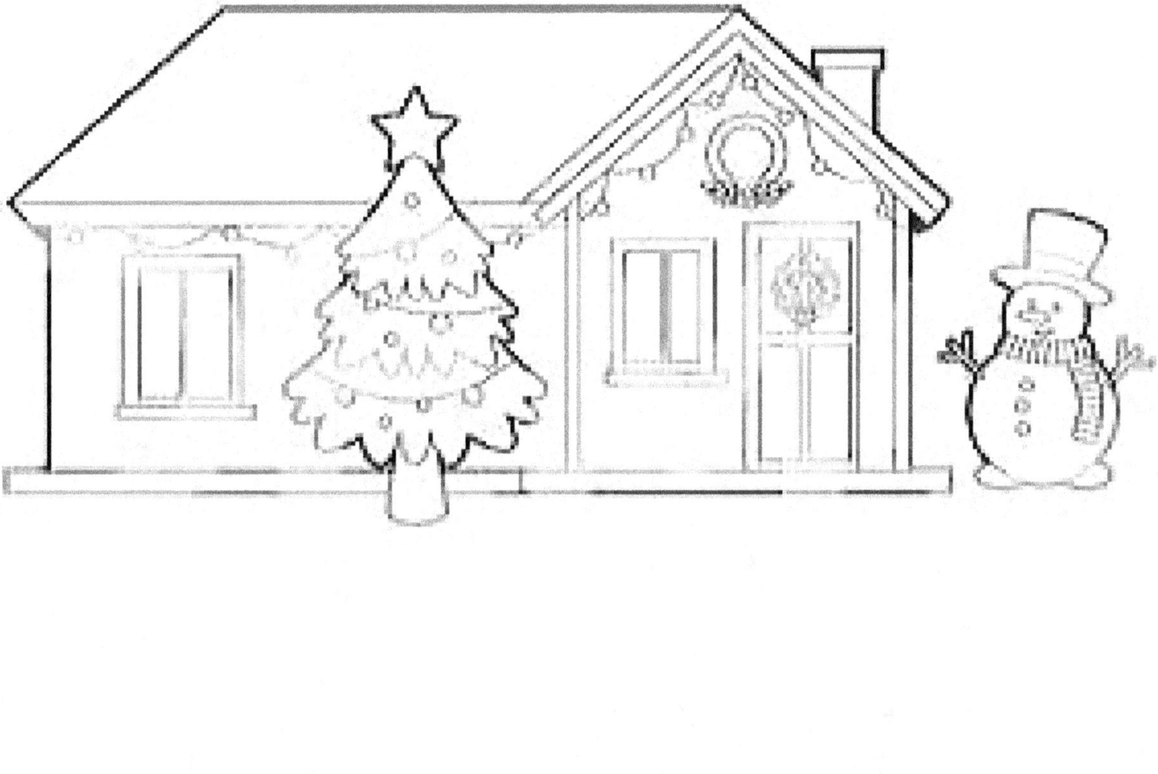

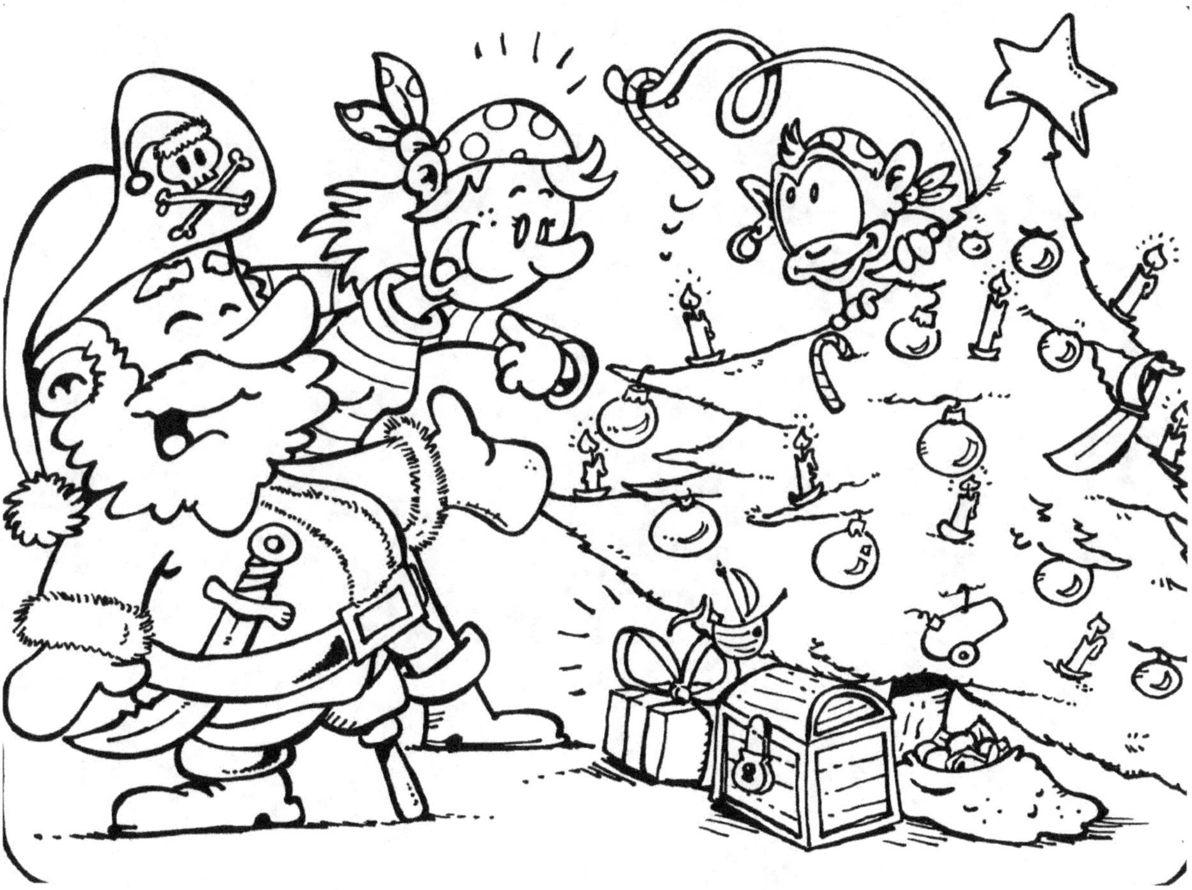

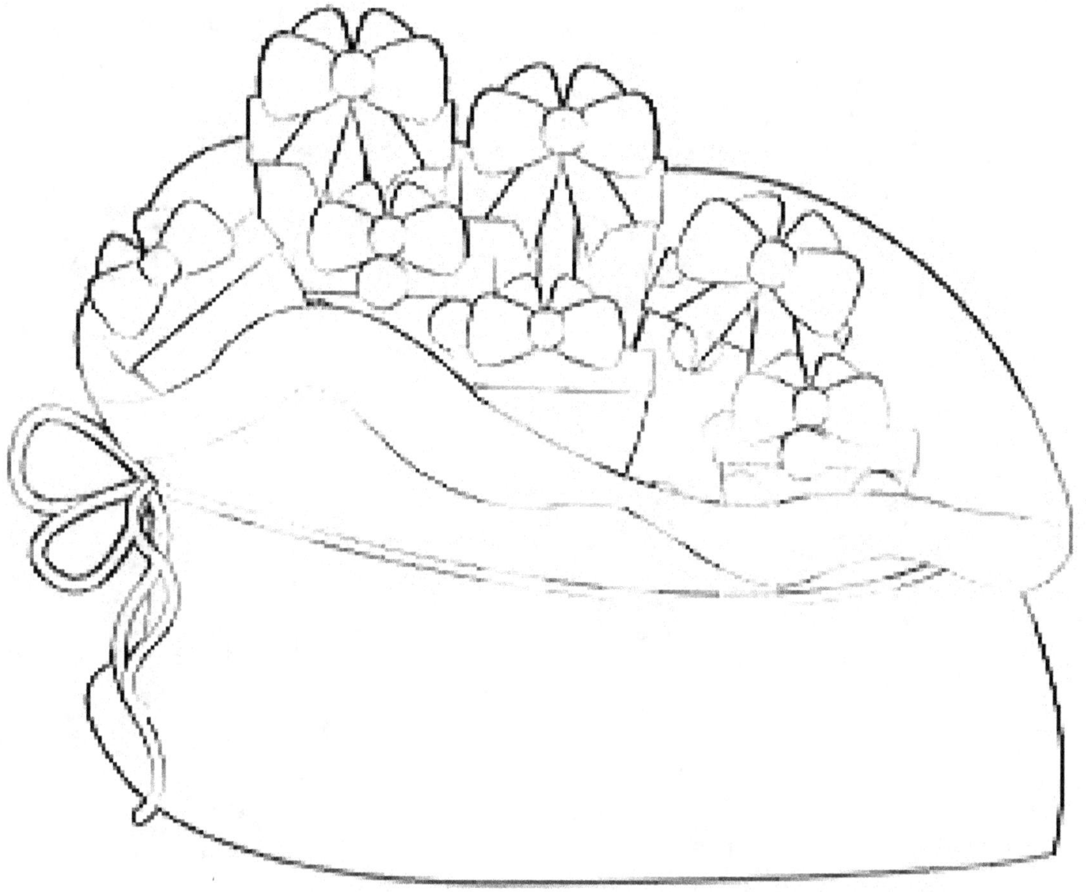

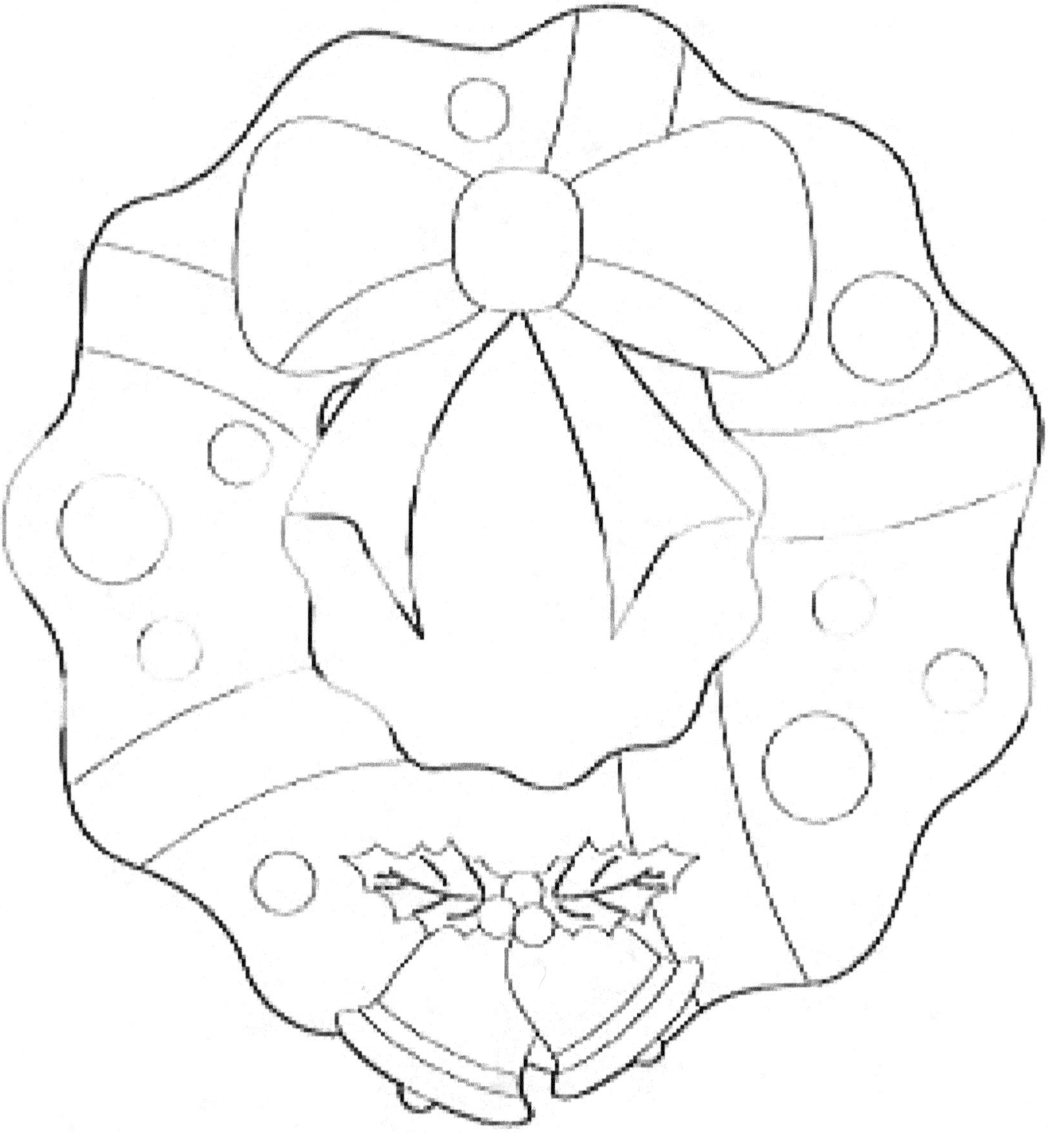

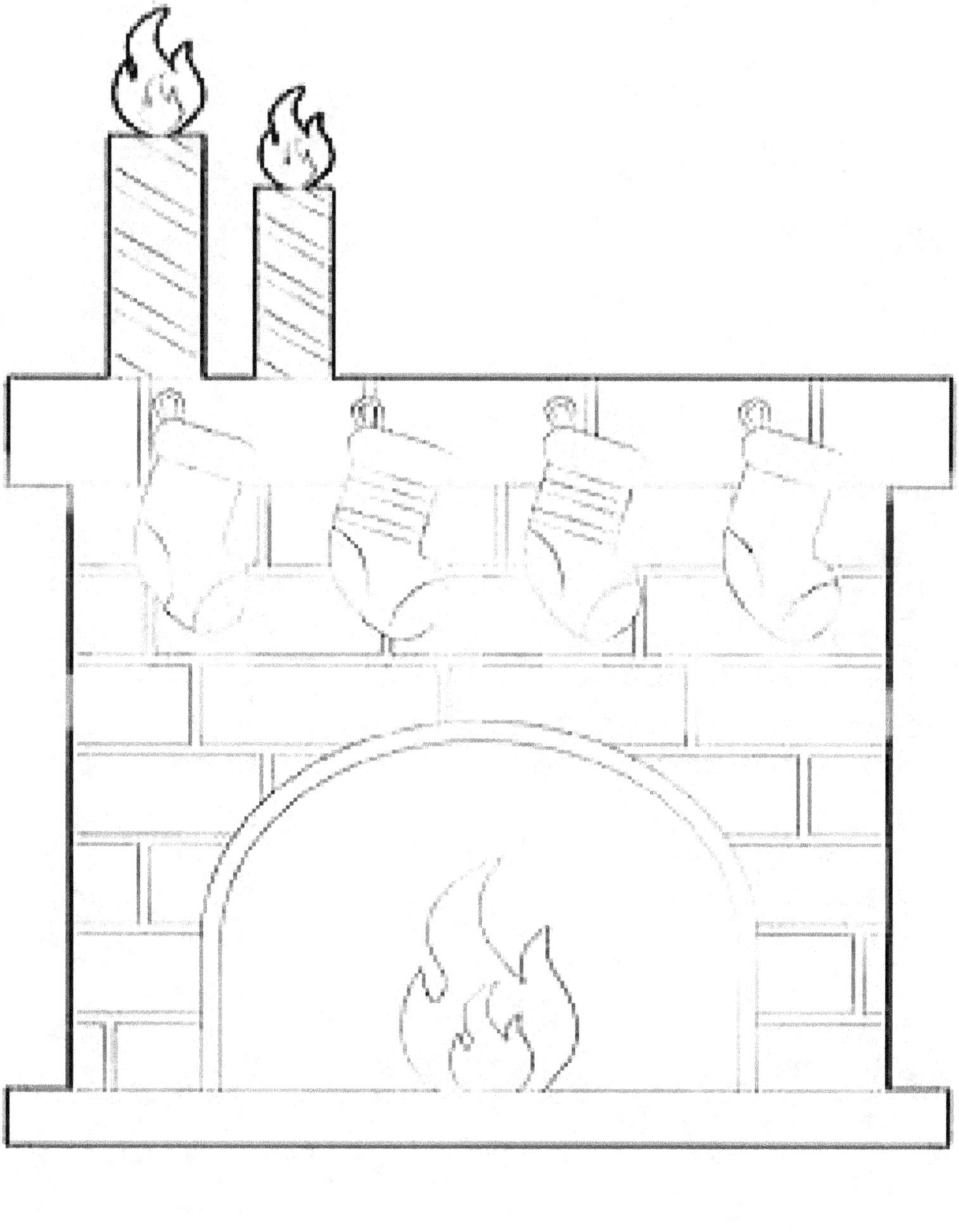

HAPPY

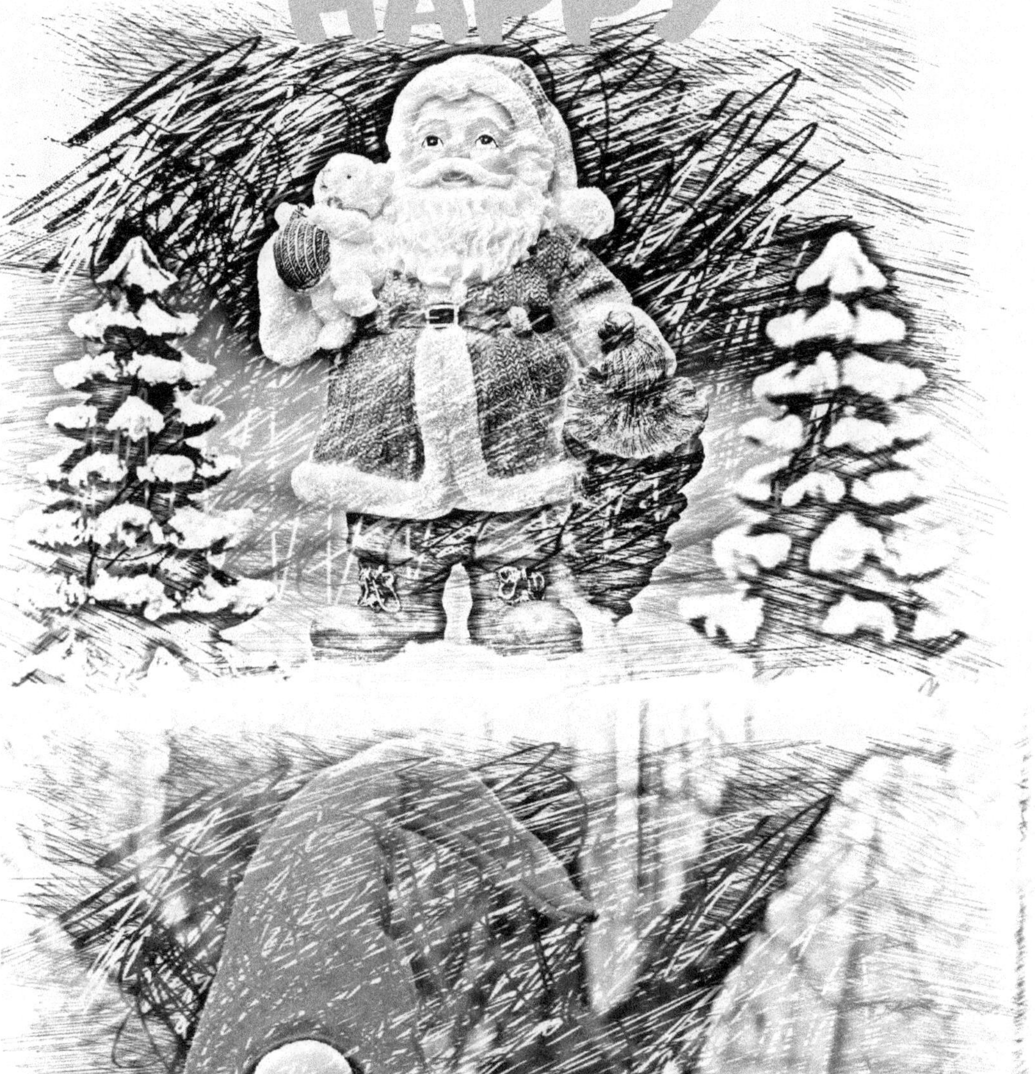

COLORING

www.ingramcontent.com/pod-product-compliance
Lightning Source LLC
Chambersburg PA
CBHW081454220526
45466CB00008B/2634